Independent Schools
Examinations Board

ENGLISH PRACTICE
EXERCISES
11+

Andrew Hammond

Editor: Ann Entwisle

Independent Schools
Examinations Board

www.galorepark.co.uk

GALORE PARK

Published by ISEB Publications, an imprint of Galore Park Publishing Ltd
19/21 Sayers Lane, Tenterden, Kent TN30 6BW
www.galorepark.co.uk

Design and typography by Typetechnique, London W1
Printed by Charlesworth Press, Wakefield

ISBN: 978 0903627 69 6

First published 2008, reprinted 2009, 2010, 2011, 2012, 2013

Details of other ISEB publications and examination papers, and Galore Park
publications are available at www.galorepark.co.uk

Acknowledgements

My thanks go to the pupils of Copthorne Prep for their help in compiling this book, and for ensuring that my work, as ever, remains rooted in the reality of the classroom. Thanks are also due to Chris Jones, my Headmaster, for his continued support, to Ann Entwisle for her hawk-eyed editing, and to Nick Oulton and the Galore Park team.

The publishers wish to thank the following companies for permission to use the images:

Page 62 (TL) Matthew Richardson/Alamy; (BL) Nino Mascardi/Getty Images; (BR) INTERFOTO Pressebildagentur/Alamy
Page 63 (TL) Steppenwolf/Alamy; (BL) Paul Broadbent/Alamy; (TR) Terrance Klassen/Alamy

The publishers wish to thank the following for their permission to use the extracts used in this publication.

My Story: Battle of Britain – Harry Woods England 1939 – 1941. Text Copyright © Chris Preistley, 2002. Reproduced with the permission of Scholastic Ltd. All Rights Reserved; *The Charioteer of Delphi* by Caroline Lawrence, published by Orion Children's Books, a division of The Orion Publishing Group; Text © 2005 Hugh Montgomery. Extract from *Cloudsailors* written by Hugh Montgomery and illustrated by Liz Pyle. Reproduced by permission of Walker Books Ltd, London SE11 5HJ; *Dragon Boy* by Dick King-Smith by kind permission of A P Watt on behalf of Fox Busters Ltd; *Blitzcat* by Robert Westall, published by Macmillan's Children's Books, London, UK; *The Giant under the Snow* by John Gordon, published by Orion Children's Books, a division of The Orion Publishing Group; *Greek Heroes* by Geraldine McCaughrean, from an edition published in 2007 by Oxford University Press; *Millions* by Frank Boyce Cottrell, published by Macmillan's Children's Books, London, UK; From *Night Birds on Nantucket* by Joan Aiken, published by Jonathan Cape. Reprinted by permission of The Random House Group Ltd.; Excerpt from *Night Birds on Nantucket* by Joan Aiken. Copyright © 1966, 1994 by Joan Aiken. Reprinted by permission of Houghton Mifflin Harcourt Publishing Company. All rights reserved; *Shadowmancer* by G.P. Taylor, published by Faber and Faber Ltd; from *Shadowmancer* by G.P. Taylor, Copyright © 2003 by G.P. Taylor. Used by permission of G.P. Putnam's Sons, A Division of Penguin Young Readers Group, A Member of Penguin Group (USA) Inc., 345 Hudson Street, New York, NY 10014. All rights reserved; *Tell Me No Lies* by Malorie Blackman, published by Macmillan's Children's Books, London, UK; *The Snow Goose*, Copyright © 1941 by Paul Gallico; *The Time Machine* by HG Wells, printed by kind permission of A P Watt Ltd on behalf of The Literary Executors of the Estate of HG Wells; *My Life in Test Cricket* by Andrew Strauss, permission sought; *It Shouldn't Happen to a Vet* by James Herriot, published by Michael Joseph; *It Shouldn't Happen to a Vet* by James Herriot, US rights applied for; *Singing for Mrs Pettigrew* by Michael Morpurgo, published by Walker Books; 'Why Video Gamers Make the Best Spies' by Rhys Blakely, *The Times*, 18th October 2007; *Dawn to Dusk* by Jonathan Scott, reproduced with permission of Curtis Brown Group Ltd London on behalf of Jonathan Scott. Copyright © Jonathan Scott 1996; *Surviving Extremes* by Nick Middleton, published by Pan Macmillan, London, Copyright © Nick Middleton, 2003; *Surviving Extremes* by Nick Middleton, also by kind permission of Rupert Crew Ltd; *Surviving Extremes* by Nick Middleton, North American rights applied for; 'Nepal: Chukka-full of charm'/'Elephant in Nepal' by Rory Ross © *The Independent*, 3rd November 2007; *Life on Earth* by David Attenborough, by kind permission of the author; *Shackleton – A Beginner's Guide* by Christopher Edge, permission sought.

Contents

Introduction

The English Common Entrance Examination at 11+

What is the exam for?

This examination will help pupils get into their chosen senior school. It provides senior schools with evidence of what the pupil can achieve in English: how well they can read and understand text, and how well they can write.

It is called an '11+' Examination because it is taken in Year 6 – the academic year in which pupils reach their 11th birthday. If successful, candidates will then move to their senior schools for Year 7.

The words 'Common Entrance' indicate that it is an examination which is common to many independent schools (i.e. many pupils sit it across the country) and it is through this examination – or the 13+ version – that pupils may gain entry into senior school.

What is in the exam?

The English Common Entrance Examination at 11+ is divided into two papers:

Paper 1: Reading Comprehension

In this paper the pupil will be required to read a passage of fiction or non-fiction. It will be about a page in length and will begin with one or two lines of introduction, setting the scene and providing background information about the passage.

The passage will be followed by some questions to test your reading comprehension skills. The number of questions varies but is usually around 9 or 10. Some questions will ask for straightforward answers, for which the pupil will need to retrieve information and evidence from the passage. Others will require the pupil to think more deeply about the meaning of the passage, and respond with personal opinions, comments or deductions.

The number of marks awarded for questions varies, with one or two mark questions usually coming at the beginning of the exam, followed by the longer, more valuable questions at the end. The pupil should answer ALL of the questions to the best of their ability.

The paper is out of 25 marks in total.

Paper 2: Composition

In this paper the pupil will be asked to demonstrate their writing skills by answering ONE question from a choice of 5 or 6 composition tasks. Types of writing on offer may include (but will not be limited to):

- imaginative/story writing

- factual/personal description

- writing involving discussion/opinion/memory

- a book review

- a picture stimulus

Grammar and punctuation are important throughout, as are handwriting and spelling. The paper is out of 35 marks in total, which includes up to 10 marks for spelling, syntax and punctuation.

Part one: Comprehension

Exercise 1.1

Read the passage and answer the questions which follow, using proper sentences.

Brave Pilot
from *Battle of Britain* by Chris Priestley (2002)

The extraordinary courage of our pilots during the Second World War is recorded here in this gripping account of one expedition across the English Channel.

1   As we moved off across the grass in the early morning light, the clumsy bumping finally gave way to that great feeling of floating: dull old earth giving way to air and soaring flight. It got me every time, every single time.

Off over the rooftops and steeples, the orchards, the hedgerows in blossom, the hop
5   fields; over the cliffs and the closed-off beaches, out across the sea to the War beyond the slate-grey waters of the Channel.

We flew in tight formation and I tried to concentrate on maintaining my position as we approached the soot-black skies of Dunkirk. A huge wall of black smoke rose in front of us, a filthy cloak that turned day into night. Then a shaft of sunlight cut a slit through the
10   clouds, hitting the sea like a searchlight. In the sea there were boats and big ships and wrecks sticking out of the waves like jawbones. Near the beach the water was flecked with the floating wreckage of ships and men, the beach studded with those who were waiting for escape. It was a Bible scene, if ever I saw one. Like the Israelites at the Red Sea with Pharaoh at their back, waiting for some kind of deliverance.

15   We patrolled the coast, but though we saw plenty of action going on on the ground, we saw no sign whatsoever of the Luftwaffe, though we could see evidence of their handiwork all around. We were at the limits of our range here and we got the order to return to base before we ran out of fuel.

I have to say I felt relieved. Good, I thought, it's over and not a scratch. I banged the
20   inside of the cockpit and grinned. I'd heard of chaps in France who only went up the one time and got blasted; bang, end of story. Not me, though.

Then a Messerschmitt shot straight past in front of me, blasting away at the Spit to my starboard. Then there was another, and another. I looked wildly around me. The radio was full of shouting and swearing. 'Behind you!' someone shouted. Behind who?
25   Behind who?

Me109s were coming down on us from all over the place, dropping out of the clouds above us. I found myself ducking, ridiculously, inside my cockpit, twitching nervously as if I was being buzzed by hornets.

A sixth sense told me there was one on my tail and I lurched wildly to avoid it, almost crashing into another Spit as I did so. I decided to loop back and try and get some kind of view of what the heck was going on.

30

The sea and sky spun round together like a kaleidoscope until I righted myself. I tried to get my bearings but I couldn't see a thing. I heard someone screaming. Screaming and screaming in my headphones.

35

I looked about, craning my neck. Nothing. Then I saw it: an Me109 coming straight at me from above. I rolled away as it blasted at me. A Spit shot by, coughing smoke, with flames in the cockpit. A German aircraft following behind, blasting like fury. I fired at him but missed by miles. Debris was flying past, clipping my wing.

They were all around me but never in my gun sight. I could feel myself almost crying with the frustration of it. It just felt like sooner or later I was going to get hit and go down. They were better than me. It was as simple as that. The Spitfire might have been the better plane, but not with me in the cockpit.

40

I swung round and suddenly a Messerschmitt shot across in front of me. I fired off a quick squirt and caught the tail fin. Then there was nothing to fire at. As fast as the Germans had come they were gone, and we were left to limp back to base.

45

1. *'It got me every time. Every single time.'* (line 3)
   What do you think the pilot is referring to here? (1)

2. There is a clear difference in the landscapes and skies either side of the Channel.
   How has the author used descriptive language to highlight this contrast?
   Refer closely to the passage in your answer. (4)

3. Why does the sixth paragraph (lines 22–25) come as such a surprise to the reader? (2)

4. What do you think is meant by the term *'sixth sense'* in line 29? (2)

5. Describe, using your own words, the scene on the beaches at Dunkirk. (3)

6. *'… though we could see evidence of their handiwork all around.'* (lines 16–17)
   What is the author referring to here? (2)

7. The author uses repetition often in the passage.
   Give one example and describe its effect. (2)

8. In the second paragraph a long, complex sentence is used to describe the beginning
   of the pilot's journey. Later in the passage short sentences and phrases are used.
   How does this change in style affect the tone of the passage?
   What do you think the author was hoping to achieve? (4)

9. What impressions do you get of the pilot's character from the whole passage?
   Use evidence from the text to illustrate your opinions. (5)

[Total marks 25]

Exercise 1.2

Read the passage and answer the questions which follow, using proper sentences.

From *The Charioteer of Delphi* by Caroline Lawrence (2006)

Young Nubia hangs on tight to Urbanus, as he takes her on a chariot race around the arena.

1   As her chariot exploded out of the stalls, Nubia screamed and clutched Urbanus's waist beneath the coil of leather reins.

Entering the morning arena was like plunging into a pool of water. She was aware of the vast cool space above her and of a line of pounding horses stretching away to her left

5   and right. The chariot floor was bouncing so much that at times she was airborne.

Above the thunder of nearly two hundred hooves on the sandy trace she could barely hear what Urbanus was shouting over his shoulder.

'We all have to stay in our lanes until we reach the linea alba, that white line on the track up ahead. And then –' here he tipped his body to the left '– we can try for the

10   inside lane!' He laughed as Nubia screamed again. She had almost fallen out of the little chariot.

Now the landmarks of the central barrier were flashing by on her left: two lofty green marble columns with a row of bronze dolphins on top, an altar, a discus thrower, a spiral pillar with a statue of a winged victory, a pavilion and the massive obelisk on its square

15   base. To her right were tier upon tier of empty seats not yet illuminated by the sun.

Urbanus's whole body moved as he drove, leaning first one way, then the other, even bending forward at the waist to urge on the horses. Nubia closed her eyes for half a circuit and held tight to his lean torso in its stiff leather strapping, but the bouncing of the wicker and leather chariot made her feel sick so she opened her eyes again, just in

20   time to see the cones of the meta prima rushing up on her left. They were like three enormous bronze cypress trees planted very close together.

'Hang on,' bellowed Urbanus, 'and have a look behind to see how far ahead we are!' Leaning in, he gave a deft tug of the innermost rein with his left hand. Nubia gasped as they took the turn. They were so close to the meta that she could see the intricate

25   designs carved into the nearest cone and she could feel a breeze caused by their passage. For a sickening moment the chariot skidded sideways in a spray of sand. After a protesting squeal the wheels began to turn again as the horses regained the straight. The chariot's speed increased.

Nubia had forgotten to look around but through the monuments on the barrier she

30   caught a flash of black horses and a black-skinned driver. Lupus's team must be close behind. She could see the rest thundering behind them.

Soon they were coming up to another meta – the turning point closest to the carceres from which they had first emerged. This time Nubia knew to lean into the turn as

35 Urbanus took the chariot in a tight skidding arc. Then the wheels bit sand and then they were bouncing down the straight again. Above the sound of their own horses' hooves Nubia heard another drumming thunder and saw something out of the corner of her eye. A dark shape, two, three, four nodding horses' heads as a team of bays began to overtake them on the right.

Nubia looked over and saw that Scopas was driving.

40 He was leaning so far forward at the waist that his body was horizontal and he seemed to float. Every iota of his being was focused on his horses and on the track ahead.

Nubia gasped as Scopas' chariot hit a bump and he rose up into the air. But he came down as nimbly as an acrobat, his concentration never faltering. He might be stiff and awkward on land, but behind a team of four stallions Scopas was as lithe as a dancer.
45 She saw his left hand give a subtle twist on the two inside reins while at the same moment he touched the tip of his whip to the captain's rump. The bay team effortlessly overtook them, moved into the inside lane and – like a dancer's ribbon – flowed smoothly around the meta out of sight.

Urbanus and Nubia were left breathing Scopas' dust.

1. 'Entering the morning arena was like plunging into a pool of water.' (line 3)
   What do you think the writer means by this?

   Write down a sentence or two to explain how you interpret this simile
   (a descriptive phrase comparing one thing with another). (2)

2. Why does Nubia find it difficult to hear what Urbanus was shouting to her? (1)

3. Identify and write down the sentence from the passage which tells you that the
   arena in which they are racing is not full of spectators. (1)

4. How do you know there are many other chariots and horses in the arena?
   Refer to words or phrases in the passage in your answer. (1)

5. Identify and discuss evidence in the passage which suggests that chariot-racing
   requires great physical effort from the driver as well as from the horses. (2)

6. How do you think Nubia regards Urbanus?
   Discuss your answer as fully as you can, and with reference to the passage. (3)

7. Describe your impressions of Scopas from what you have read in the passage.
   You may like to think about: his personality; his appearance; his experience and skill. (3)

8. (a) Do you get the impression from the passage that Nubia has raced before?
       Support your answer with evidence from the text. (3)
   (b) Do you get the impression that Urbanus has raced chariots before?
       Again, refer closely to the passage in your response. (3)

9. This is an exciting account of a chariot race. Discuss the ways in which Caroline Lawrence manages to build excitement and suspense for the reader. Think about:

- action being narrated

- the characters' responses

- descriptive language

- variety of short and longer sentences. (6)

[Total marks: 25]

Exercise 1.3

Read the passage and answer the questions which follow, using proper sentences.

The Myth of the Mountainfolk
from *Cloudsailors* by Hugh Montgomery (2005)

The narrator tells how the race of Menfolk dwelled on Earth, some taking to the mountains, others to the lowlands.

1   In the beginning, far, far in the distant past, before the moon existed or time itself had come to be, the skies were of fire and black, and burned like oil on a midnight sea. But in the cold void of space, the flames were tamed and sapped of strength. And as they cooled, the Earth was born.

5   She was young and beautiful and warm, clad in pure air, and bathed in gold by the summer sun. Her mountains rose in massive black majesty, and in winter the snows that fell upon her were as white as light itself. In spring, meltwater distilled from the icicles, spilled from the peaks, and tumbled clear and clean through the rivers, tinkling like crystal against the boulders, bringing life to the plains and valleys below.

10   Amidst this beauty dwelled the Menfolk. Some settled high in the mountains in hidden caves hewn from the cliffs, clad in pelt of fox and wolf for warmth. Others lived in the lowland valleys, where they tended the fertile soil. But they were one people, and would travel from high to low, low to high, sharing the wealth of root and berry, never taking more from the Earth than she could afford to give.

15   Time passed and, slowly, the Mountainfolk and the Lowlanders each grew into the place of their dwelling, as the ivy grows inseparable from the branches of the ageing oak. The Lowlanders travelled less to the mountains, where the air was sparse and thin. And the less they climbed, the less they thought of the mountains until, one day, they were no longer able to ascend at all. Many moved from the valleys, to settle the distant coastal
20   plains. And with time, they came to forget the mountains and those who dwelled among them.

Meanwhile, the Mountainfolk above grew accustomed to the harshness of the heights, relishing the delicacy of the air, cold and fragile, and finding the heavy vapours of the lowlands ever harder to breathe. In time, they could spend no more than hours in the
25   valley floor before, coughing and weakened, they were forced to retreat. Yet food was scarce so high in the mountains, and they continued to forage among the fields and stores of the Lowlanders below. They moved at night, when the mountain slopes were frozen and safe from sudden avalanche, and when moonshadows would shield them from sight. For they were a shy and gentle people, grown fearful of the ways of the
30   Lowlanders, and anxious what discovery might bring.

And as these Mountainfolk foraged below, the night air cooled, and a thick cloud rose and lapped the shores of the mountain slopes. Under the yellow light of the rising moon, those who remained above took yeti claw and tooth and fashioned glittering coracles of ice. These they launched from ramps of snow to sail upon the sea of cloud, ferrying the returning bounty from peak to peak. But such work had to be done before dawn, before the beat of the rising sun could strike. For then the cloud became turbulent, boiling violently and spilling the unwary from their craft.

But things were changing in the Lowlanders' world. Those who had settled on the coastal plains had swelled in number, and with them their appetite for food and fuel. Their cities grew, consuming everything around them. Trees were felled, whole forests cleared. Fires burned day and night. Fumes and phosphor filled the air, thickening to a distant smear of yellow paste above the towns. And the Mountainfolk shook their heads in disbelief.

Before long the valley air became acrid, foul to the taste and cruel to the lungs of the Mountainfolk. Their descents became ever more brief, and their dwellings were abandoned as they retreated ever higher. Soon, only the strongest could descend to forage. Food became scarce. In desperation, they took to harvesting summer lichen from the rocks, drying and storing it for the winter. But this was not enough and, with time, the weak succumbed. Faced with starvation, they sought refuge in the distant mountain ranges, fleeing in a fleet of glittering ice-coracles, praying they might make landfall before sunrise.

1. What effect do you think the author has achieved by referring to the Earth as 'she'? (2)

2. Write down a sentence from the passage to show that the Menfolk had respect for the Earth in the beginning. (1)

3. (a) Identify and write down the simile (a descriptive phrase comparing one thing with another) used in the fourth paragraph. (1)
   (b) Comment on the effectiveness of this phrase. (2)

4. What caused the Lowlanders to make less frequent visits to the Mountains? What did they dislike about the higher ground? (2)

5. Describe the Mountainfolk in your own words. (2)

6. (a) Why did the Mountainfolk grow to dislike the lowlands? (2)
   (b) How were the Mountainfolk able to find food without visiting the lowland valleys? (2)

7. Write down two quotations from the passage which illustrate how the Lowlanders' respect for the Earth diminishes after a time. (2)

8. The passage is written in a mythical style. Write down two examples from the passage where the author has used the language of myths and legends. Then comment on the effectiveness of the phrases you have chosen. (4)

9. What do you think will happen between the Mountainfolk and the Lowlanders? Explain your answer with reference to the text. (5)

[Total marks: 25]

Exercise 1.4

Read the passage and answer the questions which follow, using proper sentences.

A Dragon's Diet
from *Dragon Boy* by Dick King-Smith (1993)

Knights are always difficult to digest, according to Montague the dragon.

1   The dragon opened his huge mouth, with its rows of long sharp teeth, and belched. It was not only a very loud belch, it was also visible, for it emerged in the shape of a blue flame.

'Montagu Bunsen-Burner!' cried his wife. 'Where are your manners?'

'I do beg your pardon, my dear,' replied her husband. 'It was that last knight I ate last
5   night. Tinned food never agrees with me, it is so hard to digest.'

'Then I shall have to put you on a diet,' said Mrs Bunsen-Burner. 'Nothing but sheep or swine or oxen from now on. That should be no great hardship – a bullock of goodly size is better for you than a knight, any day.'

'I know,' said Montagu. 'It's not that I really like the taste of the fellows – so metallic, you
10   know, sets my teeth on edge. It's just that they are such a confounded nuisance, forever challenging every dragon they meet, with their great long lances and their silly swords. One simply has to eat them to get a bit of peace and quiet. Yesterday's one was typical. I was having a snooze in the forest, minding my own business, harming neither man nor beast, when this damned fellow comes galloping up, shouting, "Have at thee, Fiendish
15   Worm! Thy end is nigh!" and stuff like that. Then he points his lance at me and cries, "Prepare to die!" Same to you with knobs on, I thought, and I swallowed him down and had the horse for afters.'

Montagu belched again but more discreetly, placing one scaly paw over his mouth.

'I'll warrant you did not cook the horse properly,' said Mrs Bunsen-Burner. 'You know
20   how delicate your stomach is. I'm not saying you can do much about a knight in full armour – you have to have them cold – but something the size of a charger ought to be properly barbecued. You have only yourself to blame.'

'Yes, dear,' said Montagu.

'Right then,' said Mrs Bunsen-Burner. 'No more knights until I say so. Is that understood?'

25   'Yes, dear,' said Montagu meekly.

During many years of wedlock he had learned, sometimes painfully, that it was best to give way to his wife, and it was seldom that he summoned up the courage to oppose her will, which was of iron. There was not a dragon in the length and breadth of Merrie England, he told himself, that would dare stand up to Albertina Bunsen-Burner.

30   There were ways of getting round her, however, and one, which Montagu found especially effective, was flattery.

To understand his use of it, you must realize that dragons' comments upon each other's appearance are the exact opposite of what we humans say. 'Beautiful', 'handsome', 'pretty', 'good-looking' – these are all words that any self-respecting dragon hopes never to be called, for they indicate the scorn, contempt or downright loathing of the speaker.

35

Ugliness of form and feature is what every dragon takes pride in, and a standard compliment would be one such as Montagu now paid Albertina. To give it added weight, he used his pet name for her.

'Hotlips,' he said in a sugary voice. The look in Albertina's blood-red eyes softened.

40   'Yes, Monty?' she said.

'Oh, Hotlips!' said Montagu. 'You are by far the most hideous dragon in the land!'

Albertina positively bridled. She would have fluttered her eyelashes if she had had any. 'Oh, Monty!' she said. 'You say the nicest things.'

'Yes,' said Montagu. 'I know. Now, about this diet …'

---

1. What caused Montagu to belch so loudly?   (1)

2. (a) Why might a knight taste 'metallic' (line 9)?   (1)
    (b) Does Montagu like eating knights? Give evidence from the passage to
         support your answer.   (1)

3. What do you think it means to have a will made of 'iron' (line 28).   (2)

4. Would Mrs Bunsen-Burner be pleased to be told she looked charming and radiant?
    Give reasons to explain your answer.   (2)

5. With specific reference to the passage, show how Mrs Bunsen-Burner's attitude
    towards her husband changes. How does it change, and why?   (3)

6. What have you learned about Mr Bunsen-Burner from the passage?
    Refer to evidence from the text in your answer.   (3)

7. Dragons usually appear in traditional myths and legends. What makes Dick King-Smith's
    story so different from a traditional myth? Think about tone, atmosphere, language and
    humour in the passage.   (3)

8. In the passage the author provides a refreshingly different view of dragons –
    not the usual images of ferocious beasts, feared by knights.
    How does the author help to change the way we view dragons?
    Use evidence from the passage to illustrate your comments.   (4)

9. Continue this conversation between Mr and Mrs Bunsen-Burner in your own words.   (5)

[Total marks: 25]

Exercise 1.5

Read the passage and answer the questions which follow, using proper sentences.

A Surprise Visit
from *Blitzcat* by Robert Westall (1989)

A long day at the look-out post is pleasantly interrupted by a surprising, but welcome guest.

1   He was sipping tea from his Thermos when he saw the cat limping up the turf towards him. His first thought was that black cats were lucky. But through his binoculars she didn't look very lucky. She looked thin, beaten, furtive, and her fur was staring.

    He had no feelings about cats, one way or another. But she was an event in the
5   monotony. Company. When she paused, throwing back her head to sniff, ten yards from the post, he took a pressed-beef sandwich from his packet, and sallied out to meet her. She fled, though he called to her as softly, as gently as he could. He thought bitterly that he couldn't even give a starving cat a beef sandwich properly. He tore up the sandwich and dropped the pieces on the grass and went back inside, watching her through the
10 dark slit that was so much like a bird-watcher's hide. He watched with sad satisfaction as she sniffed and ate the sandwich; then turned his attention back to the sea.

    Next thing he knew, she was up on the sandbags beside him, purring wildly, rubbing herself in ecstasy against the hand that held the binoculars. He laughed at his sudden success; his popularity. He gave her another sandwich. That, too, vanished instantly.

15 He became drunk on doing a fellow-creature good. In all this terrifying world, here was someone to whom he could make a difference. She got the rest of his lunch and tea. He had no appetite; his fear made him feel slightly sick all the time. Janet told him off when he brought back his sandwiches uneaten. He stroked the cat tentatively, horrified at the way her spine-nobbles stuck out, the sharpness of her pelvic bones.

20 'Poor old puss. You've had a hard time …'

    The cat began to purr brokenly, so softly he could hardly hear her. She sat down on the sandbags by his elbow and began to wash herself. Somehow, she made the abandoned post feel fully manned, with a proper garrison. Like home. The afternoon sun seemed warmer. The war in France not quite hopeless. The blood seemed to move in his veins
25 for the first time in a fortnight.

1. Unlike most black cats, why did this one seem unlucky? (1)

2. (a) Did the man like cats as a rule? (1)
   (b) Why was he especially pleased to see this one? (2)

3. 'He thought bitterly that he couldn't even give a starving cat a beef sandwich properly.' (lines 7–8)
   What do you learn from this sentence about how the man regards himself? (2)

4. Explain how the cat's reaction to the man changed once she had eaten his sandwich. (2)

5. 'He became drunk on doing a fellow-creature good.' (line 15)
   What do you think is meant by this sentence? (2)

6. Write down two words or phrases from the passage which give you clues that this story is set in wartime. (2)

7. Where was this man, and what do you think he was doing, before the black cat arrived on the scene? (3)

8. With close reference to the passage, show how the author has conveyed to readers the frightening atmosphere of war through the thoughts and behaviour of the main character. (4)

9. Write a short dialogue in which the man returns to Janet and tells her all about the strange visitor who came to his post that day.
   Write your conversation as a play script between the two characters. (6)

[Total marks: 25]

Exercise 1.6

Read the passage and answer the questions which follow, using proper sentences.

From *The Giant under the Snow* by John Gordon (1968)

In the middle of a forest, Jonk finds an area of land that is not all it seems …

1   Jonk looked around her. The copse was on a very low flattish mound so regularly shaped it may have covered the ruins of a small building, a temple perhaps. But several ridges splayed out from it like the spokes of a wheel, or the rays of a sun shape. Jonk counted them. Four straight ones and one shorter and bent. Not a wheel, more like a
5   gigantic hand with trees thrusting up between the fingers.

    A hand? What if it closed on her! The thought made her jerk her head up. Her hair was wet now. It hung in dark strings to her shoulders and made a spiky fringe across her forehead. Her imagination was trying to frighten her but she would not be beaten. She would circle the copse.

10   She stepped from the mound to one of the ridges, but her foot was too near the edge, and the rain-sodden earth began to crumble. She tried to jump and the extra pressure pushed a miniature landslide away beneath her and she fell full length between the fingers of the green hand. It seemed to clutch at her and she almost cried out, but a moment later she crawled clear unhurt.

15   She stood up, facing the green hand, and stooped to brush her coat. As she did so she saw something shining where the black earth had crumbled.

    The horn bleated again, nagging like Miss Stevens. It was a sudden spurt of anger more than anything else that made Jonk stride into the 'V' of the grassy ridges and stoop to pick up the glinting object. But as her hand reached for it she paused. The object was
20   like a shiny yellow ribbon, twisted in upon itself. A clutch of worms wintering under the soil? No, it was metal. She pulled a fern leaf, doubled it to make it stiff, and poke the object clear. It was circular, about the size of her palm, and was composed of metal ribbons that twisted and writhed among themselves in an endless pattern. It looked like a brooch, perhaps an old one, perhaps gold, Certainly it was a discovery; she had been
25   right to visit the temple of trees.

    She picked it up, crumbling the earth from its crevices as she turned it in her hands. There was a distinct pattern to it, and in the middle of the interwoven gilded strips was a shape like a man standing upright with his legs together and his arms outstretched. His head was a loop of metal.

30   Now she would go back. The green hand had given her a gift. It no longer seemed unfriendly. Jonk smiled slightly as she bent to brush the brooch in the grass of one of the ridges. The grass was short and fine, and beneath it the earth was spongy. She pressed it and it gave. Another landslip and more treasure?

She was about to press again when the turf dimpled, as though it was going to split of
its own accord and save her the trouble. But it did not crack. A ripple ran the length of
the ridge, and suddenly, with a soft sound almost like a sigh from underground, it
humped itself in the middle. Jonk jerked back. The movement stopped. The ridge was
absolutely still. The hump in the middle was very low and may have been there all the
time. Stooping may have made her giddy and she had imagined it. But she was afraid. She
was able to admit to herself that she was afraid. It was time to go.

35

40

1. What effect does the opening sentence of the passage have on you, as you begin
   to read it? (2)

2. Explain in your own words how the copse resembles a giant hand. (2)

3. Write down a phrase from the passage which suggests to you that someone was
   waiting for Jonk. (2)

4. How did Jonk find the brooch? What caused it to become visible to her? (2)

5. What made Jonk pause before reaching for the metal object beneath the soil? (2)

6. What have you learned about Jonk's character? Refer to evidence from the passage
   in your answer. (3)

7. 'The green hand had given her a gift. It no longer seemed unfriendly.' (lines 30–31)
   Jonk seems less afraid after finding the object. But what causes her to leave
   the copse, in fear, by the end of the passage? (3)

8. What do you think this 'temple of trees' once was? Write a few sentences to explain
   your ideas, with some reference to the words of the passage. (4)

9. Explain, in a few sentences of your own, how the author manages to bring the copse
   to life for the reader.
   Refer to actual words and phrases from the passage in your explanation. (5)

[Total marks: 25]

15

Exercise 1.7

Read the passage and answer the questions which follow, using proper sentences.

From *Greek Heroes* by Geraldine McCaughrean (2006)

In Greek mythology, King of the Gods, Zeus, wanted to create Humankind, so he began with some gold. But, as he soon discovers, Humans can be their own worst enemies …

1   The first time Zeus created Humankind, he used gold. Of course he did. Zeus had every precious substance at his fingertips, and an eye for beauty. Unfortunately the Race of Gold had an eye for beauty, too, for no sooner were they moulded and cast and buffed up to a shine than they began to prance and preen, and pride themselves on their looks.

5   'How beautiful we are! How fine! How precious! Who will treasure us? Who will admire us? Who will worship us and do our bidding?'

Zeus melted them down and ground their golden bones into dust which he sprinkled into the rivers.

The second time, he used silver. It had a ghostly loveliness and was agreeably soft within
10   his clever hands.

The Race of Silver was elegant and effete. They did not prance about or flaunt their sinuous silvery beauty. In fact they scarcely moved at all. When they were not thinking beautiful thoughts, they were gazing at spiders' webs sprinkled with dew or stroking the silky strands of each other's hair or watching their breath cloud their own shining
15   kneecaps. When they lay down and slept, they rarely woke up again.

Zeus piled hills on their sleeping forms and turned instead to bronze. The Race of Bronze was bursting with energy and needed little sleep. It was tireless and hardworking and brutally strong. It tore down spiders' webs in gathering wood for its forges, and on these forges it made spades and mattocks and hoes, armour and knives and spears.
20   Once the Race of Bronze discovered war, they were happy indeed. The fields lay fallow and the beds unslept in … for the Men of Bronze were busily slaughtering one another with mace and arrow and sword.

Zeus had no need to destroy them. They killed each other, leaving their brazen bones scattered about among the ruins of their fallen forts.

25   There was nothing left but iron. Iron and earth and clay. Rather than dirty his hands, Zeus gave the work over to Prometheus the Titan. Once, before their conquest by the Olympians, the Titans had ruled Heaven and Earth. Now Zeus could snap his fingers and the few surviving Titans were obliged to do his dirty work.

But it was a good choice. Prometheus was a master craftsman. Despite being given such
30   poor quality materials, his big hands twisted the iron into a delicate filigree of bone, and clad it in coarse clay with a topknot of grass. He lavished the tenderest care on his little manikins and grew fond of them, for all their imperfections.

> 35 When they asked *Who? When? Where?* and *What?* Prometheus taught them the Sciences. When they gazed up at him, in their innocence, and asked *Why?* he taught them the Arts – Music, Painting, Poetry, and Dance. When they shivered in their furless, goosy skin, he even climbed to the mountaintops and plucked a glimmer of Fire from the wheel of the Sun Chariot to warm Mankind.

1. Describe in your own words the characteristics of the Race of Gold. (2)

2. Do you think Zeus cared for Humankind at the beginning of their creation?
    Write down a phrase or sentence from the passage to support your answer. (2)

3. How did the Race of Silver differ from their ancestors of gold? (2)

4. What do you think the author means when she refers to the '*ghostly loveliness*'
    of silver in line 9? (3)

5. What do you think of when you hear the word *bronze?*
    In what ways do you think the Race of Bronze lived up to its name?
    Explain your answer with reference to the passage. (3)

6. Explain what you think Zeus might have learned from creating his first three
    races of humankind. (3)

7. Write down a sentence from the passage that illustrates Prometheus's feelings
    for the Race of Mankind he created. (2)

8. What have you learned from the passage about Zeus's plans for Humankind?
    How was he hoping they would turn out?
    Try to support your comments with evidence from the passage? (4)

9. Though written in prose, the passage is quite lyrical in places because the author has
    used some writing techniques often used by poets. One such technique is alliteration.
    Give two examples of alliteration in the passage and describe their effectiveness. (4)

[Total marks: 25]

Exercise 1.8

Read the passage and answer the questions which follow, using proper sentences.

A Visitor to Stay
from *Heidi* by Joahanna Spyri (1880)

High up on the mountainside Uncle Alp receives a visit from his niece, who brings some
surprising news.

1   It took nearly an hour to reach the high pasture where Uncle Alp's hut stood on a little
plateau. The little house was exposed to every wind that blew, but it also caught all the
sunlight and commanded a glorious view right down the valley. Three old fir trees with
huge branches stood behind it. Beyond them the ground rose steeply to the top of the
5   mountain. There was rich grazing land immediately above the hut, but then came a mass
of tangled undergrowth, leading to bare and rugged peaks.

Uncle Alp had made a wooden seat and fixed it to the side of the hut looking over the
valley. Here he was sitting peacefully, with his pipe in his mouth and his hands on his
knees as the little party approached. Peter and Heidi ran ahead of Detie for the last part
10   of the way, and Heidi was actually the first to reach the old man. She went straight up to
him and held out her hand. 'Hallo, Grandfather,' she said.

'Hey, what's that?' he exclaimed gruffly, staring searchingly at her as he took her hand.
She stared back, fascinated by the strange-looking old man, with his long beard and
bushy grey eyebrows. Meanwhile Detie came towards them, while Peter stood watching
15   to see what would happen.

'Good morning, Uncle,' said Detie. 'I've brought you Tobias's daughter. I don't suppose
you recognize her as you haven't seen her since she was a year old.'

'Why have you brought her here?' he demanded roughly. 'And you be off with your
goats,' he added to Peter. 'You're late, and don't forget mine.' The old man gave him such
20   a look that Peter disappeared at once.

'She's come to stay with you, Uncle,' Detie told him, coming straight to the point.
'I've done all I can for her these four years. Now it's your turn.'

'My turn, is it?' snapped the old man, glaring at her. 'And when she starts to cry and fret
for you as she's sure to do, what am I supposed to then?'

25   'That's your affair,' retorted Detie. 'Nobody told me how to set about it when she was
left in my hands, a baby barely a year old. Goodness knows I had enough to do already,
looking after Mother and myself. But now I've got to go away to a job. You're the child's
nearest relative. If you can't have her here, do what you like with her. But you'll have to
answer for it if she comes to any harm, and I shouldn't think you'd want anything more
30   on your conscience.'

Detie was really far from easy in her mind about what she was doing, which was why she spoke so disagreeably, and she had already said more than she meant to.

The old man got up at her last words. She was quite frightened by the way he looked at her, and took a few steps backward.

35 'Go back where you came from and don't come here again in a hurry,' he said angrily, raising his arm.

Detie didn't wait to be told twice. 'Goodbye, then,' she said quickly. 'Goodbye, Heidi,' and she ran off down the mountain, not stopping till she came to Dorfli.

1. Did the old man recognise Heidi when he first saw her?
   Refer to a word or phrase from the passage to support your answer. (2)

2. What relation is Detie to the young girl, Heidi? (1)

3. Do you think Heidi is pleased to see the old man?
   Write down a sentence from the passage to support your answer. (2)

4. Explain what is meant by the following sentence:
   'The old man gave him such a look that Peter disappeared at once.' (lines 19–20) (2)

5. Rewrite the following sentence in your own words, keeping the same meaning
   as far as possible: 'That's your affair.' (line 25) (2)

6. Do you think Detie feels comfortable about leaving Heidi in the care of the old man?
   Refer to the passage in your answer. (3)

7. Do you think Detie is frightened of her uncle?
   Include evidence from the passage to support your answer. (3)

8. Describe your impressions of the old man. Include any important words and phrases
   from the passage which might affect how you regard him. (4)

9. Imagine that Detie felt unable to face her Uncle with the news that Heidi was coming
   to stay. Instead she writes him a letter, which she sends with Heidi. Write this letter. (6)

[Total marks: 25]

Exercise 1.9

Read the passage and answer the questions which follow, using proper sentences.

> # Moving House
> ## from *Millions* by Frank Cottrell Boyce (2004)
>
> *Damien, his brother Anthony and his father have moved into a new house. Anthony likes to think of himself as an estate agent; Damien likes to picture himself as a saint.*
>
> ### Moving House – by Anthony Cunningham, Year Six
>
> 1   We have just moved house to 7 Cromarty Close – a three-bedroomed property, not
>   overlooked to the front. It cost £180,000 but will retain its value well or most likely go
>   up! It has solar panels on the roof and a cost-efficient central-heating system throughout.
>   It has two bathrooms, inc. en suite to the master b'room. Substantial gardens front and
> 5   rear complete the picture in an exclusive new development in a semi-rural setting. I've
>   got my own bedroom at last. It's got footballer wallpaper, which I chose myself.
>
> * * *
>
> To be architectural about it, I found the new house disappointing.
>
>   I remember Cromarty Close when it was made of string. Dad took us to a big field near
>   the railway, all overgrown with brambles and nettles. A man with a checked shirt and a
> 10   clipboard led us to a place where the brambles had been cleared and the grass cut
>   short. He pointed down one and said, 'Dogger.' Then he walked to the corner of the
>   next one and said, 'Finisterre.' Then he pointed off to the left and said, 'Cromarty'.
>
>   'What d'you think?' Dad said. 'Want to move here?'
>
>   I said, 'Yes, please!' very enthusiastically.
>
> 15   So we did.
>
>   Actually, my enthusiasm was because of a misunderstanding. I thought he was suggesting
>   we live in the field, with the string. A lot of saints have lived in unusual houses. St Ursula
>   (4th century) lived on a ship with 11,000 holy companions. St Simeon (390–459) tried
>   to avoid temptations of the world by living on top of a three-metre column. When
> 20   sightseers started coming to stare at him, he moved to a ten-metre column so he
>   wouldn't hear them. And when they just started shouting (in 449), he moved to a
>   twenty-metre column, where he ended his days in peaceful contemplation.
>
>   Compared to that, living in a field full of brambles and string seemed sensible and
>   pleasant. I was looking forward to it. When we came back, all the brambles had gone
> 25   and there was a sign saying 'Portland Meadows – exclusive, discreet, innovative', and four
>   rows of houses with very pointy roofs and funny-shaped windows. Number 7 Cromarty
>   Close is a three-bedroom detached with substantial gardens and solar panels. Anthony
>   said, 'Detached houses hold their value better and three-bedroom is the configuration
>   most sought after by most buyers. The solar panels are added value.'

1. The main passage, beginning on line 7, is written in the first person narrative – from which person's viewpoint? (1)

2. What is meant by the phrase, 'To be architectural about it' in line 7? (3)

3. What do you think the writer means by the sentence,
   'I remember Cromarty Close when it was made of string?' (line X) (3)

4. What are Dogger, Finisterre and Cromarty? (1)

5. 'my enthusiasm was because of a misunderstanding.' (line 16)
   Explain what this misunderstanding was, and how it arose. (2)

6. Compare and contrast the landscape before and after the houses were built.
   What did it look like on Damien's first visit, and how had it changed when he returned? (4)

7. Why did St Simeon live on top of a tall column? (2)

8. 'So we did.' (line 15)
   (a) Explain what the narrator is referring to here. What did they do? (1)
   (b) This is a very short paragraph. Why do you think the author has chosen to write in this way? What effect is created? (3)

9. How can you tell, from reading his short essay at the beginning of the passage, that Anthony has a keen interest in the world of estate agents?
   Refer to the passage in your answer. (5)

[Total marks: 25]

21

Exercise 1.10

Read the passage and answer the questions that follow, using proper sentences.

A Sleeping Passenger
from *Night Birds on Nantucket* by Joan Aiken (1966)

Young Nate loves to care for things. Amid harsh conditions on board the Sarah Casket, he devotes his spare time to nursing a particularly unusual patient.

1   Late in the middle watch of a calm winter's night, many years ago, a square-rigged, three-masted ship, the *Sarah Casket*, was making her way slowly through northern seas, under a blaze of stars. A bitter, teasing cold lurked in the air; frost glimmered on the ship's white decks and tinselled her shrouds; long icicles sometimes fell chiming from the spars to
5   the planks beneath. No other sound could be heard in the silent night, save, from far away, the faint barking of seals.

On the deck a child lay sleeping in a wooden box filled with straw. Sheepskins covered her warmly. Had it not been for her breath, ascending threadlike into the Arctic air, she would have seemed more like a wax doll than a human being, so still and pale did she
10   lie. Near by squatted a boy, hunched up, his arms round his knees, gravely watching over her. It was his turn below, and by rights he should have been in his bunk, but whenever he had any time to spare he chose to spend it by the sleeping child.

She had been asleep for more than ten months.

Presently a bell rang and the watches changed. Bearded sailors came yawning on deck,
15   others went below; one, as he passed the boy, called out: 'Hey, there! Nate! No sign of life yet, then?'

The boy shook his head without replying. One or two of the men said: 'Why don't you give over, boy? She'll never wake in this world.'

And one, a narrow-faced character with close-set eyes and a crafty, foxy look to him,
20   said sourly: 'Why waste your time, you young fool? If it weren't for you and our sainted captain she'd have been food for the barracootas long ago.'

'Nay, don't say that, Mr Slighcarp,' somebody protested. 'She've brought us greasy luck so far, hain't she? We're nigh as full with whale-oil as we can hold.'

'Hah!' sneered the man called Slighcarp. 'What's *she* to do with the luck? We'd have had
25   it whether we picked her up or no. I say she'd be best overboard before it changes. I've allus hated serving on a chick frigate.'

He went below, muttering angrily. Meanwhile the boy, Nate, calmly and taking no notice of these remarks, addressed himself to the sleeping child.

'Come on now, young 'un,' he said. 'It's your suppertime.'

30 One or two of the men lingered to watch him as he carefully raised the child with one arm and then, tilting a tin coffee-pot which he held in the other hand, poured down her throat a thick black mixture of whale-oil and molasses. She swallowed it in her sleep. Her eyelids never even fluttered. When the pot was empty Nate laid her down again in her straw nest and replaced the sheepskins.

35 'Blest if *I'd* care to live on such stuff,' one of the men muttered. 'Still and all, I guess you've kept her alive with it, Nate, eh? She'd have been skinny enough by now, but for you.'

'Guess I like looking after live creatures,' Nate said mildly. 'I'd been a-wanting summat to care for ever since my bird Mr Jenkins flew away in the streets of New Bedford. And Cap'n Casket says there's no more nourishing food in this world than whale-oil and

40 m'lasses. Ye can see the young 'un thrives on it, anyways; six inches she've grown since I had the feeding of her.'

1. What was it about the sleeping child particularly which prevented her from looking like a wax doll? (1)

2. Write down a word or phrase from the first passage which tells you that the boy is seriously concerned for the girl's welfare. (2)

3. The third paragraph is very short – just one sentence in length.
Why do you think the author has done this?
What effect does it have on your reading of the passage? (2)

4. What is the boy's name? (1)

5. What is meant by the phrase, '*Why don't you give over, boy?*' in lines 17–18? (2)

6. In what ways might the girl have brought the ship good luck? (2)

7. Describe Mr Slighcarp, using your own words as far as possible. (4)

8. What impressions of the boy do you get from the passage?
Write as fully as you can and with close reference to the text. (5)

9. Continue this story in your own words. Think about the language used and the atmosphere created in the passage and try to continue in the same style. (6)

[Total marks: 25]

Exercise 1.11

Read the passage and answer the questions that follow, using proper sentences.

> ### The Dark Forest
> ### from *Shadowmancer* by G P Taylor (2003)
>
> *Beadle does not like to be out walking at night, especially through a dark forest. He hangs on tight to the cloak of his master and prays that the strange thulak creatures will not get him.*
>
> 1   It was a still October night. On the cliff top the harvest was gathered in and sheaves of corn were stacked together to form peculiar straw houses. A bright silver moon shone down on a calm sea. In the distance the silhouette of the *Friendship*, a collier brig, could be seen picked out against the waves. The sails of the ship looked like the flags of a
>
> 5   small army preparing for war.
>
> The brilliance of the full moon penetrated the darkest depths of the wood that gripped the tops of the cliffs. A small, darkly clad figure in a frock coat and knee boots stumbled along, carrying a long black leather case, timidly following a tall, confident man with long flowing white hair.
>
> 10   Nearby, a fox lay hidden in the undergrowth dreaming of a fresh rabbit, when suddenly it was woken by the panic of a deer bolting from the cover of a holly bush and running deeper into the darkness of Wyke woods.
>
> 'What was that?' The small man was startled and his voice jumped and quivered. He dropped the leather case in fright and clutched at the cloaked figure that he had
>
> 15   followed so closely through the autumn night. '*It's there*,' he squealed. 'I can see it, it's in the trees.'
>
> His companion grabbed him by the ear. 'Keep quiet, Beadle. The world doesn't need to hear your voice.'
>
> The small man pinched his eyelids together as he tried to peer into the darkness and
>
> 20   hide in his companion's cloak at the same time. Beadle didn't like the darkness and he hated the night. Bravery was for other people, and the night was to be spent by the fire of the inn, listening to stories of far-away places, the news of war in other lands and of smuggling, while drinking warm, frothy beer.
>
> Here in the wood on the top of the cliff was a different world for Beadle, a world
>
> 25   where he did not belong. The wood was the place of boggles, hedge witches, hobs and *thulak*. Beadle feared the thulak more than anything. They were strange, invisible creatures of the dark. They could steal upon you at night, smother you in a dark mist and take from you the will to live. There were stories that they would creep through open windows and come into houses to cover an unsuspecting sleeping victim like a
>
> 30   dark blanket. Once the victim was seized he couldn't move. They would take his strength and fill his mind with horrifying hideous thoughts. These were the thulakian dreams that would be with him for the rest of his life. They would leave their victims

listless and heavy – limbed, with sunken eyes from the sleepless nights spent fearing their return.

35   Beadle grasped his companion's cloak even tighter as a gentle breeze rustled the brown, crisp leaves in the trees.

'Is it a man or is it … them?' He could hardly say the words; his right leg shook, his eyelids twitched, his mouth went dry and his tongue stuck to the roof of his mouth.

'Them?' hissed his companion in his face. 'Who are *them*? Can't you say the word? What
40   are you frightened of?'

Beadle hunched his shoulders and buried his face in the musty black cloak of his tall, angry companion. 'Thulak,' he whispered feebly, trying to muffle his voice so they would not hear him.

His companion raised both his hands and cupped his mouth like the bell of a trumpet;
45   he took in a deep breath and with a voice that came from the depths of his soul, he bellowed: 'Thulak. Thulak. Thulak.' The voice echoed around the woods, the fox scurried from the brush and ran deeper into the undergrowth.

A roost of the blackest rooks lifted from the trees above their heads and their *caw-caw* filled the night sky as they circled above the branches, dancing in the moonlight.

50   '… *No*,' whispered the now terrified Beadle. 'Please, Parson Demurral, don't say that word, they will hear and they will come and get us, my mother said …'

He was hastily interrupted.

'*Us*, Beadle? Did you say *us*?' Demurral towered over the cowering, frightened form of his servant. 'I fear nothing and no one, and they have every reason in the world to fear
55   me. Tonight, my little friend, you will see who I really am and you will not say a word to anyone. I control creatures that are far more frightening than the thulak. One word of what you see tonight and you will never dare to close your eyes again, or want to see the sun go down on another day. Now, come on, we have work to do; a ship awaits its fate and I await mine.'

1.   What was it that startled Beadle as he followed his companion through the forest?   (1)

2.   Beadle does not like being out in the forest at night. What would he rather be doing?   (2)

3.   Look again at the simile '*like a dark blanket*' on lines 29–30.
     Why do you think the author chose these words?
     How do they add to your impressions of the thulak?   (2)

4.   Write down three phrases from the passage which suggest to you that Beadle is frightened of the thulak.   (3)

5.   Is the Parson frightened of the thulak too?
     Support your answer with close reference to the passage.   (2)

6. '*Please, Parson Demurral, don't say that word, they will hear and they will come and get us, my mother said …*' (lines 50–51).
   What do you think Beadle would have gone on to say had he not been interrupted? Continue his speech in your own words. (3)

7. '*Tonight, my little friend, you will see who I really am …*' (line 55).
   Share your own opinion of who, or what, the Parson's real identity might be. (2)

8. What impressions do you get of the relationship between Parson Demurral and Beadle from the passage? Use evidence from the text to illustrate your comments. (4)

9. The scene in the passage is set in a dark forest. How has the author brought this location to life for the reader? Write down, and discuss, three phrases in which the author is appealing to your senses. (6)

[Total marks: 25]

Exercise 1.12

Read the passage and answer the questions which follow, using proper sentences.

From *Tell Me No Lies* by Malorie Blackman (1999)

Gemma is sitting in her bedroom, flicking through one of her many scrap books.

1   The moon and stars and rainbows on the ceiling flickered, then steadied themselves.
       Gemma glanced up unconcerned. She looked across the room to where her mother's
       scarf lay draped over the bedside lamp. The lamplight shining through the navy-blue scarf
       adorned with gold and silver planets, the moon and stars, made her room appear
5   mystical, magical.

       Gemma turned back to the scrapbook lying on her lap. The shaded lamp made the
       room dark and mysterious but there was just enough light to see by comfortably.
       Gemma stroked the lettering on the outside of the scrapbook before opening it.
       Scrapbook number seven. This book was one of her favourites and she returned to it
10   again and again. Like all her scrapbooks, it contained photographs of mums. Mums
       smiling, crying, laughing, wistful. Lots and lots and lots of mums.

       Gemma turned the page. Here, a mum with smiling eyes and untidy hair like a halo
       hugged her daughter tight, whilst the headline below the photograph yelled out,
       MOTHER SAVES CHILD FROM OVERTURNED CAR. And on the opposite page, a
15   mum standing next to a boy, her arm around his shoulders. The headline that went with
       this photograph declared, MUM FLIES OFF WITH SON FOR NEW HEART. Gemma
       only ever kept the headlines that went with her mums – never the full newspaper article
       – but she could remember the story that went with this one. This mum's son needed a
       heart and liver transplant and the doctors in Britain had all but written him off. But not
20   his mum. His mum was determined to do whatever it took to keep her son alive, so
       she'd taken him to America. And it had had a happy ending. The boy received his
       transplant and lived.

       Gemma sighed. She liked happy endings. She turned the page.

       'Don't shout at me, Dad. I'm not deaf!' Tarwin, Gemma's brother, yelled from downstairs.

25   'I'll shout at you until you start listening to what I say!' Dad ranted.

       Gemma turned to the next page.

       'I'll listen when you stop nagging me.'

       Tarwin and Dad were at it again. Every evening they had a shouting match, a contest to
       see who could raise the roof first.

30   Ah! Now here was a mum who looked lovely. She had kind, twinkling eyes. She was a
       foster mum whom everyone loved. She never said a cross word to or about anyone –
       not that any of her neighbours could recall at any rate – and the children she fostered
       always turned out fine, with nothing but praise and love for their new mum. She'd

even received an award on the telly. Gemma thought wistfully of the children this
woman had looked after. She imagined coming home from school, opening the front
door to be greeted with a kiss and a hug. Gemma smiled. If she closed her eyes, she
was almost there.

1. Explain how the moon and stars are projected onto Gemma's ceiling. (2)

2. Describe in your own words the atmosphere in Gemma's bedroom. (2)

3. What does Gemma keep in her scrapbooks? (1)

4. Give one example of a mother's courageous act which features in the passage. (1)

5. (a) What have you discovered about Gemma's personality from the passage? (2)
   (b) What have you learned about Tarwin's personality from the passage? (2)

6. Write a few sentences comparing and contrasting the atmosphere inside Gemma's
   room with the atmosphere downstairs, where her brother and father are. (3)

7. Write down a sentence from the passage which tells you that Tarwin and his
   father often argue in this way. (2)

8. In as much detail as possible, and with close reference to the passage, suggest a
   possible reason for Gemma's unusual collection. (4)

9. (a) Describe your feelings towards the character, Gemma. (2)
   (b) Show how the author has made you feel this way. Give examples from the
       passage of particular phrases or sentences which have influenced the way
       you feel about Gemma. (4)

[Total marks: 25]

Exercise 1.13

Read the passage and answer the questions which follow, using proper sentences.

From *The Snow Goose* by Paul Gallico (1941)

In a wild and lonely part of the Essex coast there lives a hermit who has only the birds for company.

1   The Great Marsh lies on the Essex coast between the village of Chelmbury and the
ancient Saxon oyster-fishing hamlet of Wickaeldroth. It is one of the last of the wild
places of England, a low, far-reaching expanse of grass and reeds and half-submerged
meadowlands ending in the great saltings and mud flats and tidal pools near the
5   restless sea.

Tidal creeks and estuaries and the crooked, meandering arms of many little rivers
whose mouths lap at the edge of the ocean cut through the sodden land that seems to
rise and fall and breathe with the recurrence of the daily tides. It is desolate, utterly
lonely, and made lonelier by the calls and cries of the wildfowl that make their homes in
10   the marshlands and saltings – the wild geese and the gulls, the teal and widgeon, the
redshanks and curlews that pick their way through the tidal pools. Of human habitants
there are none, and none are seen, with the occasional exception of a wild-fowler or
native oyster-fishermen, who still ply a trade already ancient when the Normans came
to Hastings.

15   Greys and blues and soft greens are the colours, for when the skies are dark in the long
winters, the many waters of the beaches and marshes reflect the cold and sombre
colour. But sometimes, with sunrise and sunset, sky and land are aflame with red and
golden fire.

Hard by one of the winding arms of the little River Aelder runs the embankment of an
20   old sea wall, smooth and solid, without a break, a bulwark to the land against the
encroaching sea. Deep into a salting some three miles from the English Channel it runs,
and there turns north. At that corner its face is gouged, broken and shattered. It has
been breached, and taken for its own the land, the wall, and all that stood there.

At low water the blackened and ruptured stones of the ruins of an abandoned
25   lighthouse show above the surface, with here and there, like buoy markers, the top of a
sagging fence-post. Once this lighthouse abutted on the sea and was a beacon on the
Essex coast. Time shifted land and water, and its usefulness came to an end.

Lately it served again as a human habitation. In it there lived a lonely man. His body was
warped, but his heart was filled with love for wild and hunted things. He was ugly to
30   look upon, but he created great beauty. It is about him, and a child who came to know
him and see beyond the grotesque form that housed him to what lay within, that this
story is told.

It is not a story that falls easily and smoothly into sequence. It has been garnered from
many sources and from many people. Some of it comes in the form of fragments from

1.   'It is one of the last wild places in England ...' (lines 2–3)
     What do you think the author means by this?
     Describe the kind of place he is referring to.   (2)

2.   Why do you think the author has used the word *restless* to describe the sea in line 5?
     Is it an effective description?   (2)

3.   Name two natural features which run through the Great Marsh to the open sea.   (2)

4.   What do you think the word 'bulwark' means in line 20? Read the sentence in which
     it appears, and others around it, to help you identify its meaning.   (2)

5.   Rewrite the following sentence in your own words, retaining the same meaning:
     'Lately it served again as a human habitation.' (line 28)   (2)

6.   From the evidence available in the passage, give a possible explanation for the title
     of this story, The Snow Goose.   (2)

7.   This is the opening passage to Paul Gallico's story and it serves as a long introduction
     to its main character, Rhayader, who lives on the marsh.
     How has the author developed the readers' sympathies and affection for this man?
     Refer to actual quotations from the passage in your answer.   (2)

8.   What have you learned about the sea from reading this passage?
     How has the author brought it to life?   (5)

9.   The passage makes us think of a harsh and inhospitable landscape.
     How has the author created this impression for us? Refer to words and phrases
     from the passage to support your answer.   (6)

[Total marks: 25]

Exercise 1.14

Read the passage and answer the questions which follow, using proper sentences.

The Magical Feeling of Flying
from *Five Children and It* by E Nesbit (1902)

How does it feel to fly? Here are some children who find out.

1 'I wish we all had beautiful wings to fly with.'

The Sand-fairy blew himself out, and next moment each child felt a funny feeling, half heaviness and half lightness, on its shoulders. The Psammead put its head on one side and turned its snail's eyes from one to the other.

5 'Not so dusty,' it said dreamily. 'But really, Robert, you're not quite such an angel as you look.' Robert almost blushed.

The wings were very big, and more beautiful than you can possible imagine – for they were soft and smooth, and every feather lay neatly in its place. And the feathers were of the most lovely mixed changing colours, like a rainbow, or iridescent glass, or the
10 beautiful scum that sometimes floats on water that is not at all nice to drink.

'Oh – but can we fly?' Jane said, standing anxiously first on one foot and then on the other.

'Look out!' said Cyril; 'you're treading on my wing.'

'Does it hurt?' asked Anthea with interest; but no one answered, for Robert had spread his wings and jumped up, and now he was slowing rising in the air. He looked very
15 awkward in his knickerbocker suit – his boots in particular hung helplessly, and seemed much larger than when he was standing in them. But the others cared but little how he looked – or how they looked, for that matter. For now they all spread out their wings and rose in the air. Of course you all know what flying feels like, because everyone has dreamed about flying, and it seems so beautifully easy – only, you can never remember
20 how you did it; and as a rule you have to do it without wings, in your dreams, which is more clever and uncommon, but not so easy to remember the rule for. Now the four children rose flapping from the ground, and you can't think how good the air felt running against their faces. Their wings were tremendously wide when they were spread out, and they had to fly quite a long way apart so as not to get in each other's way. But
25 little things like this are easily learned.

All the words in the English Dictionary, and in the Greek Lexicon as well, are, I find, of no use at all to tell you exactly what it feels like to be flying, so I will not try. But I will say that to look *down* on the fields and woods, instead of *along* them, is something like looking at a beautiful live map, where instead of silly colours on paper, you have real
30 moving sunny woods and green fields laid out one after the other. As Cyril said, and I can't think where he got hold of such a strange expression, 'It does you a fair treat!' It was most wonderful and more like real magic than any wish the children had had yet. They flapped and flew and sailed on their great rainbow wings, between green earth and

blue sky; and they flew right over Rochester and then swerved round towards
35 Maidstone, and presently they all began to feel extremely hungry. Curiously enough, this
happened when they were flying rather low, and just as they were crossing an orchard
where some early plums shone red and ripe.

They paused on their wings. I cannot explain to you how this is done, but it is
something like treading water when you are swimming, and hawks do it extremely well.

40 'Yes, I daresay,' said Cyril, though no one had spoken. 'But stealing is stealing even if
you've got wings.'

'Do you really think so?' said Jane briskly. 'If you've got wings you're a bird, and no one
minds birds breaking the commandments. At least, they may *mind*, but the birds always
do it, and no one scolds them or sends them to prison.'

45 It was not so easy to perch on a plum-tree as you might think, because the rainbow
wings were so *very* large; but somehow they all managed to do it, and the plums were
certainly very sweet and juicy.

Fortunately, it was not till they had all had quite as many plums as were good for them
that they saw a stout man who looked exactly as though he owned the plum-trees,
50 come hurrying through the orchard gate with a thick stick, and with one accord they
disentangled their wings from the plum-laden branches and began to fly.

1. Why are the children's wings compared to '*scum that sometimes floats on water*'
   in line 10? How could they be similar to such a thing? (1)

2. How, according to the writer, could we all know what flying feels like? (2)

3. The writer says that there are no words to describe the feeling of flying.
   What effect does this statement have on the reader?
   How does it affect your opinion of flying? (3)

4. Explain in your own words what is meant by the following sentence:
   '*They paused on their wings.*' (line 38) (2)

5. Read Cyril's remarks on lines 40–41 once again. According to the text, no one had
   actually spoken at this point, so why did he say this? What did he assume the
   others were thinking? (3)

6. How does Jane try to justify taking the plums? Why, according to her, would it be
   alright on this occasion for them to take the fruit? (2)

7. What made the children suddenly take off from the orchard? (2)

8. Throughout the passage, the writer creates a strong impression that flying is a wondrous, magical experience. Identify and discuss two phrases or sentences from the passage which you found particularly effective in creating a sense of wonder. (4)

9. Imagine you are one of the characters in the story. Narrate this scene from your own point of view, using the first person narrative. You may like to consider: how it felt when your wings first appeared; how you felt when you began to fly; the sweet taste of the fruit; the surprise of seeing the sudden appearance of the stout man approaching. (6)

[Total marks: 25]

Exercise 1.15

Read the passage and answer the questions which follow, using proper sentences.

Journey through Time
from *The Time Machine* by H G Wells (1895)

The time traveller begins to reveal the extraordinary story of his adventure.

1   'I am afraid I cannot convey the peculiar sensations of time travelling. They are
    excessively unpleasant. There is a feeling exactly like that which one has upon a
    switchback – of a helpless headlong motion! I felt the same horrible anticipation, too, of
    an imminent smash. As I put on pace, night followed day like the flapping of a black wing.

5   The dim suggestion of the laboratory seemed presently to fall away from me, and I saw
    the sun hopping swiftly across the sky, leaping it every minute, and every minute marking
    a day. I supposed the laboratory had been destroyed, and I had come into the open air. I
    had a dim impression of scaffolding but I was already going too fast to be conscious of
    any moving things. The slowest snail that ever crawled dashed by too fast for me. The

10 twinkling succession of darkness and light was excessively painful to the eye. Then, in
    the intermittent darkness, I saw the moon spinning swiftly through her quarters from
    new to full, and had a faint glimpse of the circling stars. Presently, as I went on, still
    gaining velocity, the palpitation of night and day merged into one continuous greyness;
    the sky took on a wonderful deepness of blue, a splendid luminous colour like that of

15 early twilight; the jerking sun became a streak of fire, a brilliant arch, in space, the moon
    a fainter fluctuating band; and I could see nothing of the stars, save now and then a
    brighter circle flickering in the blue.

    The landscape was misty and vague. I was still on the hillside upon which this house
    now stands, and the shoulder rose above me grey and dim. I saw trees growing and

20 changing like puffs of vapour, now brown, now green: they grew, spread, shivered, and
    passed away. I saw huge buildings rise up faint and fair, and pass like dreams. The whole
    surface of the earth seemed changed – melting and flowing under my eyes. The little
    hands upon the dials that registered my speed raced faster and faster. Presently I noted
    that the sun-belt swayed up and down, from solstice to solstice, in a minute or less, and

25 that, consequently, my pace was over a year a minute; and minute by minute the white
    snow flashed across the world, and vanished, and was followed by the bright, brief green
    of spring.

    The unpleasant sensations of the start were less poignant now. They merged at last into
    a kind of hysterical exhilaration. I remarked, indeed, a clumsy swaying of the machine, for

30 which I was unable to account. But my mind was too confused to attend to it, so with a
    kind of madness growing upon me, I flung myself into futurity. At first I scarce thought of
    stopping, scarce thought of anything but these new sensations. But presently a fresh
    series of impressions grew up in my mind – a certain curiosity and therewith a certain
    dread – until at last they took complete possession of me. What strange developments

35 of humanity, what wonderful advances upon our rudimentary civilisation, I thought, might

not appear when I came to look nearly into the dim elusive world that raced and
fluctuated before my eyes! I saw great and splendid architecture rising about me, more
massive than any buildings of our own time, and yet, as it seemed, built of glimmer and
mist. I saw a richer green flow up the hillside, and remain there without any wintry
40   intermission. Even through the veil of my confusion the earth seemed very air. And so
my mind came round to the business of stopping.'

1. Explain how the speaker came to see the sun 'hopping swiftly across the sky' (line 6).
   Why should he be able to see such a thing? (2)

2. What was comical about the sight of the snail? (2)

3. What caused the speaker to suffer a pain in his eyes? (1)

4. Describe the colours which flash past the speaker's eyes as he speeds through time. (3)

5. Write down the sentence from the passage which tells you that the time traveller
   has not physically moved at all. (2)

6. How does the architecture of the future differ from the buildings which the
   time traveller is used to seeing? (3)

7. 'I saw a richer green flow up the hillside and remain there without any wintry intermission.'
   (line 39).
   What do you think this means? (2)

8. Describe, in as much detail as you can and with reference to the passage, how the
   narrator's feelings about time travelling change during the course of his journey. (5)

9. What impressions do you get of the speaker's character from this passage?
   Give as much detail as you can and support your comments with evidence
   from the passage. (5)

[Total marks: 25]

Exercise 1.16

Read the passage and answer the questions which follow, using proper sentences.

From *Coming into Play – My Life in Test Cricket* by Andrew Strauss (2006)

England cricketer, Andrew Strauss, describes the moment when he first realised he was in the national squad.

1 There are many ways in which England cricketers learn of their selection. Some have received congratulatory phone calls from a selector, other are tipped off by an indiscreet journalist. Most, however, have realised their fate via the radio or television. I became aware of my selection for the one-day legs of the 2003/04 winter tours of
5 Bangladesh and Sri Lanka during the morning session of Middlesex's final championship match of the season against Nottinghamshire.

Middlesex had secured their place in the following season's first division and the game was drifting along when suddenly the Test and one-day squads appeared on each of the electronic scoreboards at Lord's. I was aware of the imminent announcement, and felt
10 I had a good chance of being selected, but it still came as a huge shock when I saw my name on the list. I was overwhelmed with excitement, and I found it ridiculously difficult to concentrate on the game I was playing in. My team-mates congratulated me and the members complimented me on my selection as I walked off the field and through the Long Room for lunch. It was a strange feeling. I felt that I was ready and had done
15 enough to be selected but it was still unbelievably rewarding to gain recognition, and to realise all the years of hard work had been worthwhile.

Hearing of your selection is obviously a very special moment but it is only when your England kit begins to arrive that the enormity of what you have achieved starts to sink in. Once selected you move in the 'England bubble' and there is a constant supply of
20 goods being delivered to your house. Mobile phones, blazers, bags – it was like being a kid at Christmas all over again. Best of all was receiving my England shirts. When I opened the parcel containing them I could not stop smiling. There they were, authentic, England shirts with STRAUSS, 14, ENGLAND on the back. I could not take my eyes off them. It was brilliant. I had arrived.

25 My parents were absolutely thrilled. When I was at school they had never seriously believed that I would make a career out of cricket. They initially considered it to be a bit of fun and something I would drift away from before getting a job in the City. As I made my way at Middlesex, however, they gradually warmed to the idea of their son being a professional cricketer. They were understandably proud and pleased that I had stuck at
30 my cricket and worked diligently. The progress to where I was now had not always been smooth and there had been times when I had found cricket a little tedious. But in all our eyes my choice of career had seemed worthwhile.

1. Give three ways in which cricketers may learn of their selection for the national team. (3)

2. Why did Andrew Strauss find it so difficult to concentrate on his game? (2)

3. When he first heard of his selection, Strauss was delighted, but when did he finally realise he was in the team for real? (1)

4. What do you think the writer means by the phrase 'the England bubble' (line 19)? (2)

5. Describe, in your own words, the young cricketer's reaction to seeing his own England shirts for the first time. (2)

6. (a) Why do you think his parents did not seriously believe that he would make a career out of cricket? (2)
   (b) What did they think he would actually do for a job? (1)

7. Which qualities had Andrew Strauss shown in his career to date which had particularly impressed his parents? (2)

8. 'there had been times when I had found cricket a little tedious.'
   (a) Rephrase this sentence in your own words. (2)
   (b) Suggest possible reasons why Strauss should find cricket tedious from time to time. (2)

9. What have you learned from the passage about Andrew Strauss's:
   (a) commitment to the game of cricket? (2)
   (b) personality and qualities? (4)
   Refer to evidence in the passage in your answers.

[Total marks: 25]

Exercise 1.17

Read the passage and answer the questions which follow, using proper sentences.

From *It Shouldn't Happen to a Vet* by James Herriot (1972)

Country vet, James Herriot, finds time to admire some Yorkshire views and reflect on how he came to be working on the moors.

1   I had been away for only two weeks but it was enough to bring it home to me afresh
    that working in the high country had something for me that was missing elsewhere. My
    first visit took me up on one of the narrow, unfenced roads which join Sildale and
    Cosdale and when I had ground my way to the top in bottom gear I did what I so often
5   did – pulled the car on to the roadside turf and got out.

    That quotation about not having time to stand and stare has never applied to me. I
    seem to have spent a good part of my life – probably too much – in just standing and
    staring and I was at it again this morning. From up here you could see away over the
    Plain of York to the sprawl of the Hambleton Hills forty miles to the east, while behind
10   me, the ragged miles of moorland rolled away, dipping and rising over the flat fell-top. In
    my year at Darrowby I must have stood here scores of times and the view across the
    plain always looked different; sometimes in the winter the low country was a dark
    trough between the snow-covered Pennines and the distant white gleam of the
    Hambletons, and in April the rain squalls drifted in slow, heavy veils across the great
15   green and brown dappled expanse. There was a day, too, when I stood in brilliant
    sunshine looking down over miles of thick fog like a rippling layer of cotton wool with
    dark tufts of trees and hilltops pushing through here and there.

    But today the endless patchwork of fields slumbered in the sun, and the air, even on the
    hill, was heavy with the scents of summer. There must be people working among the
20   farms down there, I knew, but I couldn't see a living soul; and the peace which I always
    found in the silence and the emptiness of the moors filled me utterly.

    At these times I often seemed to stand outside myself, calmly assessing my progress. It
    was easy to flick back over the years – right back to the time I had decided to become
    a veterinary surgeon. I could remember the very moment. I was thirteen and I was
25   reading an article about careers for boys in the Meccano Magazine and as I read, I felt a
    surging conviction that this was for me. And yet what was it based upon? Only that I
    liked dogs and cats and didn't care much for the idea of an office life; it seemed a frail
    basis on which to build a career. I knew nothing about agriculture or about farm animals
    and though, during the years in college, I learned about these things I could see only one
30   future for myself; I was going to be a small animal surgeon. This lasted right up to the
    time I qualified – a kind of vision of treating people's pets in my own animal hospital
    where everything would be not just modern but revolutionary. The fully equipped
    operating theatre, laboratory and X-ray room; they had all stayed crystal clear in my
    mind until I had graduated MRCVS.

How on earth, then, did I come to be sitting on a high Yorkshire moor in shirt sleeves and wellingtons, smelling vaguely of cows?

1. Write down a phrase or sentence from the passage which tells you that the author feels homesick when he is away from North Yorkshire. (2)

2. James Herriot has stood in this place many times and observed how the weather can change the appearance of the landscape.
   Give two examples of the weather creating a very different view for the author. (2)

3. The author compares the clouds of fog to layers of cotton wool.
   (a) Do you think this is an effective simile? Share your opinion.
   (b) Can you think of an alternative simile which could be used in the same sentence? (2)

4. What do you think the author means when he says the fields 'slumbered in the sun' (line 18)? (2)

5. When, and how, did the author decide he wanted to become a veterinary surgeon? (2)

6. James Herriot had always wanted to become a vet.
   Why then should he be surprised to find himself 'on a high Yorkshire moor in shirt sleeves and wellingtons, smelling vaguely of cows' (lines 35–36)? (2)

7. Do you think the author is pleased to be living and working in North Yorkshire?
   With reference to the passage, show how readers are made aware of Herriot's affection for the county. (4)

8. Write down all the things which you have learned about James Herriot from the passage. (5)

9. Imagine James Herriot was interviewed about his career plans whilst at veterinary college.
   What might he have said in reply?
   Write down a response which he might have given to the question 'What will you do when you graduate from university?' (4)

[Total marks: 25]

Exercise 1.18

Read the passage and answer the questions that follow, using proper sentences.

> ### A Story-teller Explains
> ### from *Singing for Mrs Pettigrew, a Story-maker's Journey*
> ### by Michael Morpurgo (2006)
>
> *Famous children's author, Michael Morpurgo, reflects on how, and why, he became a writer.*
>
> 1   'Explain yourself, Morpurgo.' I was asked to do this quite often when I was at school. The trick, of course, was to come up with an excuse that would get me out of trouble. I became rather good at this, I think, probably because I had to be. It was a question of survival, a very necessary technique that most of us have had to master in our time.
>
> 5   In this book I am not excusing myself, but I am trying to explain myself, to understand why and how I write what I do. I shall try to explain myself to myself and in so doing will, I hope, explain myself to you.
>
> Why trouble? Why should a writer seek to explain his craft to his readers? What's the point? Surely the stories themselves are all you need? Surely it's through reading these
> 10   that we can come to an understanding of a writer's mind and methodology? That would seem to be true. It should be sufficient. This is why you will find in this book more stories than anything else. However, there are those who would like to probe a little deeper, who are not happy simply to gaze at the field of ripe corn dancing in the breeze and wonder. They want to understand how a single grain of corn grows, from where the
> 15   seedcorn comes, how it is planted and fertilized, how the earth cradles it, how the sun and rain sustain it. Perhaps this insight can lead to a more profound appreciation of the stories themselves, but more importantly it may give the reader the idea that this process of story-making and story-telling is for everyone, that we all of us have the seedcorn of stories inside us, that it is simply a question of planting it and encouraging it
> 20   to grow.
>
> I am a grower of stories. I farm them as surely as a farmer does his corn. I am a weaver of dreams, a teller of tales. I have, through my mother reading to me, through my own reading, through inspired teachers, through my great mentors Robert Louis Stevenson, Ted Hughes and Sean Rafferty, through years of practice, discovered my way of doing it.
> 25   Every writer's way is unique, I am sure, though perhaps we all have much more in common than we believe. My way will not be the only way, but it is my way, and I hope it might be interesting and maybe even useful and encouraging to tell the story of how I became the writer I am.

1. What was Morpurgo usually trying to achieve when explaining himself at school? (1)

2. What is the purpose of his explanations this time? (2)

3. 'In this book I am not excusing myself, but I am trying to explain myself,' (line 5).
   What, do you think, is the difference? (2)

4. What do you think the storyteller means by the phrase, 'I am a weaver of dreams,'
   in lines 21–22? Explain your answer as fully as you can. (3)

5. Name two different kinds of people who helped Morpurgo to find his own
   way of writing. (2)

6. What do you learn from the passage about Michael Morpurgo? Try to focus not
   only on his occupation, but also on his personality, both as a boy and in later life. (3)

7. In the final passage, the author says, 'we all have much more in common than we believe.'
   What do you think writers might have in common? (3)

8. What kind of skills do you think a successful storywriter needs? Try to use
   Morpurgo's comments from the passage as evidence to support your own answer. (4)

9. Imagine that Michael Morpurgo receives a letter from a young reader who is interested
   in becoming a writer and wants to know if it is a rewarding and enjoyable job.
   Write Morpurgo's response. (5)

[Total marks: 25]

Exercise 1.19

Read the passage and answer the questions which follow, using proper sentences.

Double Agents Wanted
from 'Why video gamers make the best spies', The Times,
18 October 2007

You have probably seen many advertisements and trailers on computer games; but have you ever seen one from MI5? You might be surprised.

1 British intelligence agencies are to offer video gamers hooked on espionage-inspired adventures the chance to live out their fantasies.

Government Communications Headquarters (GCHQ), the surveillance arm of the intelligence services, will this month become the first spy agency to embed adverts for
5 new recruits inside computer games.

The advertisements will appear as billboards in the fictional landscapes of games including Tom Clancy's Splinter Cell: Double Agent. They will not be written into the games themselves but will be fed into games when they are played on personal computers and Microsoft Xbox 360 consoles that are connected to the internet.

10 Double Agent, published by the Paris-based Ubisoft, stars Sam Fisher, an American spy who has 'little time for polite niceties and even less for lies'. Fisher works for Third Echelon, a fictional hush-hush unit of the US National Security Agency, described as 'an elite team of strategists, hackers, and field operatives.'

A spokesperson for GCHQ described the potential recruits that it wanted to reach as
15 'computer-savvy, technologically able, and quick thinking.'

'We find increasingly we have to use less conventional means of attracting people … to go beyond glossy brochures and milk-round stalls.'

Industry figures suggest that the adverts will reach a mostly male audience, aged from 8–34. GCHQ hopes to 'plant the idea in the heads of young players' of pursuing a career
20 in the secret services.

'We will monitor the results from this campaign and are ready to change our recruitment methods,' the spokeswoman said. 'We know we can't stand still.'

The move into video games demonstrates how the intelligence agencies have moved away from old-boy networks. This summer MI5 advertised for staff on the sides of
25 London buses.

But adrenaline-addicted video game junkies should be aware. GCHQ, which works on signal intelligence (hi-tech eavesdropping) and information assurance (protecting government information from hackers and other threats), is concentrating on recruiting software experts. Most will work from the agency's main listening post, in Cheltenham,
30 and will be nowhere near any James Bond-style exploits.

1. Where will the advertisements for new recruits be placed? (1)

2. In your own words, explain the meanings of the following phrases, found
   in line 15 of the passage:
   (a) computer-savvy
   (b) technologically able
   (c) quick thinking (3)

3. What do you think the GCHQ spokeswoman means by the phrase 'We know we
   can't stand still' (line 22)? (2)

4. Placing recruitment posters in unusual places is not new for the intelligence agencies.
   Where has MI5 advertised before? (1)

5. Why might some video gamers be disappointed if they sign up for a career as
   a secret agent, like James Bond? (2)

6. Having read the whole passage, can you now explain how the opening paragraph
   might be misleading for interested readers? (3)

7. Why do you think GCHQ might wish to recruit video gamers in the first place? (4)

8. In what ways has the writer of this article dramatised this story to make it more
   exciting for readers? Refer to words and phrases in the passage to support
   your comments. (4)

9. Write a short advertisement – of approximately 100 words – setting out the kind of
   skills GCHQ are looking for in their new recruits, and why young people should apply. (5)

[Total marks: 25]

Exercise 1.20

Read the passage and answer the questions which follow, using proper sentences.

Man's Closest Relative
from *Dawn to Dusk* by Jonathan Scott (1996)

Nature photographer and writer, Jonathan Scott, gets close to a family of chimpanzees, and realises we're not so different from each other.

1   Whatever I might have expected, my first glimpse of the chimps was just as exciting as everybody had predicted it would be. It was an hour or more since we had started to hike up the steep valley, and my shirt was sodden from the exertion. As we topped the rise we found ourselves at the edge of a clearing in the *miombo* woodland. Charlotte

5   pointed ahead of her to where Freud lay watching our approach.

        Freud is Fifi's eldest son; now twenty-five years old, he is currently the alpha male of the Kasakela community. He lay totally relaxed, with one foot crossed over his leg and one arm cupped behind his head. It was uncanny. But perhaps the most startling revelation came when I looked into his eyes. It was like meeting the gaze of another human being

10   – questioning, expressive, inquiring. When you look into the eyes of a buffalo or an antelope there is little sense of inquiry or recognition, no feeling that they see in the way we do. But a chimpanzee looks to see what you are doing. Freud's eyes were the colour of hazel-nuts and glistened with a familiar knowingness. They were quite different from the eyes of any other animal I had seen.

15   I had only just started to get over the excitement of seeing Freud, when Fifi appeared, accompanied by her two youngest offspring, Faustino and Ferdinand, and followed by one of her daughters and another infant. Fifi stopped to let Ferdinand climb off her back and lay down in the grass next to Freud, who began to groom her. Suddenly little Ferdinand walked towards me and grabbed me by the hand, tugging at it. I have always

20   tried to distance myself from the idea of wild animals as pets, much as I love the companionship of my own domestic cats and dogs. But that moment of unsolicited contact between myself and the young chimp totally entranced me – not because the chimpanzees seemed almost human in many of the things they did, but simply because it underlined for me that we humans are just as much a part of the natural world as

25   they are.

1. Did Jonathan Scott's first encounter with the chimpanzees live up to expectations? Refer to evidence from the passage to support your answer. (2)

2. Identify and write down a phrase from the first paragraph which tells you that the writer felt hot and sweaty after his long climb. (1)

3. Describe, in your own words as far as possible, the location where Jonathan Scott found the chimpanzees. (2)

4. 'It was uncanny.' (line 8)
   What was uncanny? What is the writer referring to here? (2)

5. In what ways, according to the writer, is a chimpanzee's gaze similar to that of a human's? (3)

6. Rewrite the following line from the passage in your own words, retaining as much of the original meaning as you can:
   'glistened with a familiar knowingness.' (line 13) (2)

7. Jonathan Scott tells us that the moment of contact between Freud and himself 'totally entranced' him (line 22). Explain what you think he means by this, and how this experience may have affected the way he views animals and humans. (4)

8. What impression do you get from this passage about the writer's appreciation for wild animals? If you were to ask him why he likes to study nature, what do you think he would say? (4)

9. Imagine you are Jonathan Scott. You have been asked to write a short article for a magazine in which you share your thoughts about how similar chimpanzees and humans really are, and how we should all view our relationships with animals. (5)

[Total marks: 25]

Exercise 1.21

Read the passage and answer the questions which follow, using proper sentences.

Because it is there
from 'We choose to go to the Moon' speech by John F. Kennedy
(12 September 1962)

Addressing an audience of university students, President Kennedy shares his plan for an historic expedition to the Moon.

1   'The Mariner spacecraft now on its way to Venus is the most intricate instrument in the history of space science. The accuracy of that shot is comparable to firing a missile from Cape Canaveral and dropping it in this stadium between the 40-yard lines.

Transit satellites are helping our ships at sea to steer a safer course. Tiros satellites have
5   given us unprecedented warnings of hurricanes and storms, and will do the same for forest fires and icebergs.

We have had our failures, but so have others, even if they do not admit them. And they may be less public.

To be sure, we are behind, and will be behind for some time in manned flight. But we do
10   not intend to stay behind, and in this decade, we shall make up and move ahead.

The growth of our science and education will be enriched by new knowledge of our universe and environment, by new techniques of learning and mapping and observation, by new tools and computers for industry, medicine, the home as well as the school ...

... To be sure, all this costs us all a good deal of money. This year's space budget is three
15   times what it was in January 1961, and it is greater than the space budget of the previous eight years combined. That budget now stands at $5,400 million a year – a staggering sum, though somewhat less than we pay for cigarettes and cigars every year. Space expenditures will soon rise some more, from 40 cents per person per week to more than 50 cents a week for every man, woman and child in the United States, for we have
20   given this program a high national priority – even though I realize that this is in some measure an act of faith and vision, for we do not now know what benefits await us. But if I were to say, my fellow citizens, that we shall send to the moon, 240,000 miles away from the control station in Houston, a giant rocket more than 300 feet tall, the length of this football field, made of new metal alloys, some of which have not yet been invented,
25   capable of standing heat and stresses several times more than have ever been experienced, fitted together with a precision better than the finest watch, carrying all the equipment needed for propulsion, guidance, control, communications, food and survival, on an untried mission, to an unknown celestial body, and then return it safely to earth, re-entering the atmosphere at speeds of over 25,000 miles per hour, causing heat about
30   half that of the temperature of the sun – almost as hot as it is here today – and do all this, and do it right, and do it first before this decade is out – then we must be bold.

I'm the one who is doing all the work, so we just want you to stay cool for a minute. [laughter]

35 However, I think we're going to do it, and I think that we must pay what needs to be paid. I don't think we ought to waste any money, but I think we ought to do the job. And this will be done in the decade of the Sixties. It may be done while some of you are still here at school at this college and university. It will be done during the terms of office of some of the people who sit here on this platform. But it will be done. And it will be done before the end of this decade.

40 And I am delighted that this university is playing a part in putting a man on the moon as part of a great national effort of the United States of America.

Many years ago the great British explorer George Mallory, who was to die on Mount Everest, was asked why did he want to climb it. He said, 'Because it is there.'

Well, space is there, and we're going to climb it, and the moon and the planets are
45 there, and new hopes for knowledge and peace are there. And, therefore, as we set sail we ask God's blessing on the most hazardous and dangerous and greatest adventure on which man has ever embarked.'

1. List two ways in which satellites in space are helping us on Earth. (2)

2. How will the growth of science and education in America be enriched, according to President Kennedy? (2)

3. (a) How much was the space budget in January 1961? (1)
   (b) The new budget is considerably greater, but still less than the country's annual expenditure on cigarettes and cigars. Why do you think Kennedy uses this comparison? (2)

4. Why should all this new investment in space exploration be 'an act of faith and vision' (line 21)?
   What do you think Kennedy means by this phrase? (2)

5. Kennedy's aims for the space programme are laid out in one very long sentence in the sixth paragraph. Why do you think he has done this?
   What effect might this part of the speech have on his audience? (2)

6. How is this effect on his audience altered by the next paragraph? (2)

7. Discuss why you think Kennedy has chosen to refer to George Mallory's expedition. How does this inclusion add to his speech and the message within it? (2)

8. This is a typically passionate and persuasive speech from a man famous for his ability to inspire an audience.
   Which parts did you find particularly powerful? Write down – and discuss – three phrases or sentences which made a strong impression on you. (6)

9. What do you think was the purpose of this speech? Include evidence from the passage to support your explanation. (4)

[Total marks: 25]

Exercise 1.22

Read the passage and answer the questions which follow, using proper sentences.

A World of Plants
from *Surviving Extremes* by Nick Middleton (2003)

Explorer and travel writer, Nick Middleton, treks through a tropical forest, and finds it is very different to the forests he knows back home in Britain.

1　　We reached the village of Bomassa and fell into our beds, hungry for sleep, rising too early the following morning for the next leg of our journey: a bumpy truck ride and another pirogue* along a smaller, winding river before we took to our feet. Finally, I was actually entering the forest.

5　　It was darker and cooler beneath the trees as we forged our way into this strange world ruled by plants. It was a world pervaded by stillness, without wind, not even a breeze, as saplings silently struggled to find a way to the sky between the solid tree trunks. The forest floor was littered with large dead leaves and flat, leathery seed cases the shape of footprints. They were grey-brown and looked as if someone had discarded

10　thousands of old insoles.

　　　We followed a path, constructed by elephants Patrick told me, which sounds as if the hike was easy-going. But a tropical forest path is not quite the same as a path through a forest where I come from. Looking ahead as I walked, there was clearly a way through the foliage, but the ground was a confusion of obstacles lying in wait to trip the unwary.

15　Roots riddled the trail, snaking across the path to snatch at my toes, and fallen branches lurked to graze my shins. Whole tree trunks lying across the track had to be clambered over in brief shafts of welcome sunlight. And as soon as I had tuned in to the obstructions at my feet, an aerial contingent took over to hinder me. Head-high creepers and vines reached out like tentacles to scratch my face or garrotte me.

20　Towards the end of our trek the hidden sky arrived from beyond the towering canopy, heralding its presence with thunder that sounded like great doors slamming in the clouds and huge boulders rolling in heaven. They rumbled and tumbled with unnatural volume, bigger than any boulders you could ever see. Immense flashes of lightening followed the deafening crashes, enough to make me jump in disbelief. I heard the rain

25　before it reached me, the trees of the forest being so densely packed that drops falling on the canopy took minutes before they reached the ground. But once they'd started to filter through, they came tumbling down into the jungle in a cascade of water that drenched me in seconds.

　　　The final stretch before the research camp meant wading through a waist-deep river. I

30　was exhausted, sodden, scratched and bruised, but we'd arrived. I truly felt as if I'd penetrated the heart of darkness.

　　　pirogue – long and narrow canoe

---

1. Write down the phrase from the first paragraph which tells you that Nick Middleton felt very tired at the end of his first day travelling. (1)

2. Why should a path constructed by elephants 'sounds as if the hike was easy-going' (lines 11–12)? (2)

3. In what ways does this forest path differ from the paths the writer is used to exploring in the forests back home? (2)

4. The author tells us that the roots were 'snaking across the path' (line 15).
   (a) What do you think he means by this? (2)
   (b) What effect is created by this metaphor? (2)

5. To what does Nick Middleton liken the thunder? (2)

6. How did the author know that the rain was on its way? Refer closely to the passage in your answer. (2)

7. 'I truly felt as if I'd penetrated the heart of darkness.' (lines 30–31)
   (a) What do you think the author means by this? (2)
   (b) What does this sentence tell you about his feelings at the end of the trek? (2)

8. The author appeals to the reader's senses throughout the passage.
   Which senses are particularly aroused, and how? Use quotations from the passage to illustrate your answer. (4)

9. Do you get the impression from the passage that Nick Middleton enjoyed his forest trek? Support your comments with close reference to the text. (4)

[Total marks: 25]

Exercise 1.23

Read the passage and answer the questions which follow, using proper sentences.

Elephant Trek
from *'Nepal: Chukka-full of charm'*, *The Independent*, 3 November 2007

Reporter Rory Ross enjoys an unusual trek through the jungle of south-east Nepal – on the back of an elephant.

1   There's no finer way of seeing the jungle than from 12 feet up, on top of an elephant. Whether bulldozing through the undergrowth, climbing hills or fording rivers, elephants walk at exactly the right speed: any faster and you'd miss something; any slower and time would hang heavily. So there I was, riding through the jungle of south-east Nepal on

5   a four-ton female elephant named Ram Kali. With me sat a look-out boy, while the manhout, or driver, straddled Ram Kali's neck, and steered by tickling her ears with his toes. Ahead of us was Chan Chan Kali, a colleague of Ram Kali's.

We were on safari in the Royal National Chitwan Park, an ark of rare and exotic fauna. As the sun set, colourful animals emerged to have a stretch and a quick drink from the

10   river Rapti, which snakes through the park. Thanks to the soundlessness of an elephant's gait, we startled kingfishers, lapwings, deer, eagles, golden oriole, and a rhinoceros with her two-month-old baby.

The scenery, suffused with soft, pink evening light, was such that you wonder why you tolerate 21st century Britain. Chitwan is a vast stretch of pristine jungle, forest and

15   flood plain, just north of the Indian border. As I looked ahead at Chan Chan Kali – the picture of pachyderm contentedness, trampling a passage through the 25-foot-high elephant grass, tail swishing, ears flapping and trunk darting out to grab clumps of vegetation – I felt blissfully secure, and could easily contemplate going feral there for a few months.

20   'Hut-hut-hut!' The look-out boy on Ram Kali suddenly became agitated. 'Hut-hut-hut!' The mahout responded by whacking Ram Kali on the head with a stick, making a sickeningly resonant thud. As Ram Kali and Chan Chan Kali lumbered ahead at full speed, the shouting look-out boy and the mahout began to jump up and down. I expected to see a tiger ready to pounce, but everything around us seemed absolutely

25   tranquil, except for the ground shaking as Ram Kali and Chan Chan Kali put on an impressive turn of speed.

A quarter-mile behind us, I saw the cause of the panic. We were being stalked, not by a tiger, but by another elephant, a wild bull elephant built like a tank, with fork-lift tusks. It was doing a feeble impersonation of a pachyderm pretending not to be following us. 'The

30   bull might charge us, tear us off the back of Ram Kali, gore us with tusks, remove our heads as if they were grapes, trample us and throw us in the river,' said the look-out.

We forded the Rapti River and double-backed along the opposing bank. The bull looked increasingly disgruntled, but for appearance's sake continued along his path, while we went in the opposite direction. We truncated the afternoon's safari, and headed home.

1. How many people are riding on the elephant? (1)

2. Why do you think the writer describes the Royal National Chitwan Park as an 'ark' (line 8)?
   What effect is created by this word? (2)

3. Rewrite the following phrase in your own words, keeping to the original meaning intended by the author:
   'which snakes through the park'. (line 10) (2)

4. What caused the kingfishers, lapwings and other creatures in the park to be startled? (1)

5. Why should the scenery in the park cause you to 'wonder why you tolerate 21st century Britain' (lines 13–14).
   What is the author suggesting here? (3)

6. Why is the phrase 'fork-lift tusks' (line 28) such an effective description? (2)

7. Describe the atmosphere on the journey before AND after the disturbance caused by the bull elephant. Refer to the passage in your answer. (3)

8. What have you learned about the writer, Rory Ross, from this passage? You may like to think about his character, any likes and dislikes which he may have, and the kind of adventures he enjoys. Write as much as you can and refer to the passage wherever possible, to support your comments. (5)

9. Write a short advertisement which might appear in a newspaper, advertising safari holidays in the Royal National Chitwan Park. Use evidence in the passage to help you describe the exciting experiences tourists could enjoy. (6)

[Total marks: 25]

Exercise 1.24

Read the passage and answer the questions which follow, using proper sentences.

From Fish to Frogs
from *Life on Earth* by David Attenborough (1979)

Most of us have seen frogs from time to time, but we might be surprised to find how clever they are if we stop and take a closer look …

1   From the beginning of their history, the amphibians were hunters, preying on the worms, insects and other invertebrates that had preceded them on to the land. They remain so today despite the appearance of bigger and more powerful hunters which have compelled them to be more circumspect in their behaviour. Some indeed are still quite formidable.

5   The horned toad of South America has a gape so big that it can with ease engulf nestling birds and young mice. But no amphibian can truthfully be described as nimble and for hunting they have to rely on something other than agility – their tongue.

The extendable tongue is an amphibian invention. No fish ever had one. It is attached not to the back of the mouth as ours, but to the front. In consequence, the frogs and

10   toads can stick it out much further than we can, simply by flicking it forward – a useful talent for a rather slow-moving hunter without a neck. Its end is both sticky and muscular so that a toad can use it first to grasp a worm or a slug and then to carry it bodily back to the mouth.

Many amphibians, including the horned toad, have very serviceable rows of teeth on

15   their jaws, as their ancestors had, but these are used for defence or as a way of gripping the prey. They do nothing to break up the food into easily swallowed gobbets or to tease out the hard inedible bits. No amphibian can chew. This is the reason why toads, when they seize one end of a worm, methodically rake the length of it with their forefeet to remove any bits of sticks or earth that might be stuck to it. The tongue

20   helps the process of swallowing by producing a lot of mucus which lubricates the food and prevents it scratching the delicate membranes of the throat. The tongue also assists in moving the food back along the floor of the mouth. So, it seems, do the eyes. All frogs and toads blink when they swallow. Their eye-sockets have no bony floor, so when they blink, the eye-balls are drawn down into the skull and make a bulge in the roof of the

25   mouth which squeezes the lump of food to the back of the throat.

The amphibian's eyes are fundamentally the same in structure as those of their fish ancestors. Optically such eyes work just as well out of water as in it. The only modification needed to make them operate efficiently in air is some means of keeping their surface clean and smooth, so the amphibians developed the capacity to blink and a

30   membrane that they can draw across the front of the eyeball.

The equipment they use to perceive sound waves in the air is, however, quite new. The fish's method of receiving sound through their bodies, amplified in some instances by the

resonance of the gas-filled swim-bladder, does not work efficiently in air, so most frogs
and toads have developed eardrums. These detect sound vibrations in the air very
35   efficiently indeed.

1.   Why should a young mouse fear the horned toad of South America?   (1)

2.   Explain the meaning of the following line from the passage, using your own words:
     '*no amphibian can truthfully be described as nimble.*' (line 6)   (2)

3.   (a) How is a frog able to stick its tongue out much further than we can?
          What is so special about its design?   (2)
     (b) Why should this prove useful to the frog?   (2)

4.   Explain in your own words the extraordinary way in which the frog's eyes can help it
     swallow its food.   (2)

5.   The frogs' eyes are the same as their fish ancestors', with one exception, which allows
     them to see clearly when out of the water. What is it?   (2)

6.   Although frogs and toads have teeth, they are not used for chewing up food into
     manageable pieces for swallowing. So how do these amphibians manage to prevent food
     from scratching their delicate throats?   (2)

7.   Unlike amphibians, fish do not have eardrums. Explain how they are able to hear.   (2)

8.   Having read the passage, has your impression of what frogs and toads are like altered
     at all? Explain your answer with reference to the passage.   (4)

9.   Frogs are descended from fish, but they have evolved significantly over time to be
     truly amphibious. Summarise in a few sentences of your own how frogs differ from
     their fish ancestors.   (6)

[Total marks: 25]

Exercise 1.25

Read the passage and answer the questions which follow, using proper sentences.

The Road to the Pole
from *Shackleton – A Beginner's Guide* by Christopher Edge (2002)

Famous explorer, Sir Ernest Shackleton, and his brave team, suffer further setbacks on their expedition across the frozen wastes of Antarctica, towards the South Pole.

1   After all the preparations for the southern trek were completed and the depots laid along the southern road, Shackleton's team set out in bright sunshine on 29 October 1908. With the ponies pulling the sledges, the men traipsed on foot, averaging over 24 kilometres a day in the first month out. By the end of November they had travelled 480
5   kilometres down the road to the Pole.

However, such rapid progress was not without its costs. In the biting cold of Antarctica the ponies suffered, the ice froze on their exposed bodies and their hooves became wounded by the jagged edges of the sastrugi ridges. At night, while the men camped safely in their tent, the ponies were left standing shivering under woollen blankets,
10   virtually unprotected from the howling Antarctic winds that swept over the ice cap. Shackleton's diary recorded their suffering, '… the ponies struggling gamely … had to plough through truly awful surface.'

On 21 November, the pony Chinaman could go no further as the terrible ice surface had crippled his legs. The ponies Grisi and Quan's strength gave out days later. To spare
15   their suffering the ailing ponies were shot. Their failing was a mixed blessing for the men, as more of the heavy burden of hauling fell upon them, but the meals of fresh pony meat helped to keep scurvy at bay.

… By December the party had passed through Scott's furthest point south and reached a huge glacier leading through the Transatlantic Mountains. Shackleton named this the
20   Beardmore Glacier after his generous expedition backer. The surface underfoot became dangerous as many crevasses littered their path. The remaining pony, Socks, was harnessed to a sledge loaded with equipment and supplies as Wild led it up the glacier. Suddenly, a crevasse opened up beneath Socks and the pony plummeted through the ice to its death. Wild fell back into the newly opened crevasse and only his quick reactions
25   saved him as he clung to the edge, before he was swiftly rescued by the others. The sledge, with its cargo of valuable food and fuel, was miraculously saved as the force of Socks's fall had shattered the wooden bar that attached the pony to the sledge.

Shackleton and his men could now rely only on their own strength and fortitude to conquer the treacherous Beardmore Glacier. As they scaled the glacier, the increasing
30   altitude and terrible snowblindness both took their toll on the group. Every step forward was dogged by the fear of deadly crevasses, as their feet constantly broke through the surface of the ice, with only the harnesses that linked them to the sledge saving them from oblivion.

Christmas Day 1908 saw the men camped at 86° South, 2,850 metres up the glacier.
35 Shackleton allowed them all a celebratory feast consisting of an increased ration of hoosh, topped with a minute portion of plum pudding, a spoonful of brandy and a restorative cigar. Even in times of extreme mental stress and physical strain, Shackleton worked hard to maintain the morale of his men and create an oasis of normality in the alienating wastes of Antarctica.

1. In line 6, the author describes the cold as 'biting'.
   What effect does this word create? (2)

2. Describe two ways in which the cold affected the ponies. (2)

3. How do you know from the passage that Shackleton was not the only explorer to journey across the frozen wastes of Antarctica? (1)

4. Why did Shackleton choose to name the glacier the Beardmore Glacier? (2)

5. What do you think the word 'crevasse' (line 23) means? (2)

6. Although the pony, Socks, was lost in the fall, how was it that the sledge it was pulling survived? (3)

7. Explain what is meant by the following words:
   ' … Shackleton worked hard to maintain the morale of his men…' (lines 37–38) (2)

8. What impression do you get from the passage of Shackleton's leadership qualities?
   Answer as fully as you can, and with close reference to the text. (5)

9. Write a short entry in Shackleton's expedition diary, for Christmas Day 1908.
   Write approximately half a page. (6)

[Total marks: 25]

Part Two: Composition

The following exercises are grouped into themed sections. The actual examination will include a variety of questions with often one question taken from each of the sections. These are typical examples and are phrased as in the examination, e.g. Choose ONE of the following. You will, of course, try them all for plenty of practice.

Exercise 2.1: Imaginative writing

1. Write a short story using ONE of the following titles:
    (a) Run for Cover!
    (b) Friend or Foe?
    (c) My River Adventure   (25)

2. Write a short story or piece of descriptive writing which begins with ONE of the following sentences:
    (a) As my eyes adjusted to the darkness, I could make out a mysterious shape in the corner.
    (b) As the wind picked up, and the sky turned an ominous black, Michael knew it was now or never.
    (c) Through the carriage window, she could see her parents slowly shrinking into the distance, their faces wreathed in white steam.   (25)

3. Write about one of the following places in an imaginative way:
    (a) A disused railway station
    (b) A mountain summit
    (c) A market   (25)

4. Describe a place which you have visited where you felt relaxed and carefree.   (25)

5. Write a descriptive paragraph which contains ONE of the following lines:
    (a) We took shelter under the dripping tree.
    (b) I turned my face towards the black sky.
    (c) There she was, soaring over the roof tops.   (25)

6. Write a story which contains the following sentence:
    'Until that moment, Jane had never once thought of going back to England.'   (25)

Exercise 2.2: Personal recounts and descriptions

1. Parents can be so embarrassing! Has there ever been a time when either your mother or your father has embarrassed you in public?
   Describe this event from your perspective AND then try to describe it from your parent's point of view. (25)

2. Have you ever been on a holiday which turned out to be disappointing?
   Describe this holiday, and how your hopes and expectations were let down. (25)

3. Write an essay on any ONE of the following topics:
   (a) My first day at school
   (b) My first victory
   (c) My first solo (25)

4. Describe the occupation you would least like to do when you are older, and explain why. (25)

5. Recommend one of the following to a class-friend. Think about why this place or product might appeal to a child of your age:
   (a) My favourite holiday destination
   (b) My best video game
   (c) My favourite film (25)

6. Have you ever been accused of something you did not do?
   Describe the circumstances which led to the accusation, and how you felt at the time. (25)

Exercise 2.3: Discursive and persuasive writing

1. 'Pets are pointless.'
    Do you agree? Do you think pets serve a purpose? Or should animals live with
    animals, and humans live with humans?
    Write persuasively in favour of, **or** in opposition to, keeping animals as pets.　　　(25)

2. Do you think the summer holidays are too long?
    Write a discussion piece in which you describe the views on BOTH sides of
    the argument.　　　(25)

3. Write a persuasive speech **either** supporting **or** opposing ONE of the following
    motions:
    (a) This House believes girls and boys should not attend the same schools.
         Co-educational schools should be abolished.
    (b) This House believes that all police officers on our streets today should be
         equipped with handguns.
    (c) This House believes that the millions of pounds spent on space exploration
         every year should be spent on feeding the world's starving people. We should
         get this planet in order before we begin exploring new ones.　　　(25)

4. Write a letter to a school magazine, persuading other children to get involved in
    after-school clubs and activities.　　　(25)

5. Write a discussion text, explaining some of the differing views on ONE of the
    following public issues:
    (a) Fox hunting
    (b) Keeping animals in captivity
    (c) The Monarchy　　　(25)

6. Share your own opinion on the following statement:
    'An obsession with health and safety today has meant that children can no longer
    have any fun outside.'　　　(25)

Exercise 2.4: Writing about books

1. Books can offer us imaginary places into which we may escape.
   Have you ever read a story in which the setting was so inviting that you wished you could travel there?
   Describe the story and its setting. (25)

2. Have you ever read a book which you just couldn't put down?
   What was it about the story which made it so appealing? (25)

3. Write a book review for a story you have read recently which surprised you. (25)

4. Write a book recommendation aimed at children your age for ONE of the following books:
   (a) My favourite action story
   (b) My favourite fantasy story
   (c) My favourite story about sport (25)

5. Many people enjoy reading autobiographies and biographies of famous people.
   Have you ever read one which you could recommend to other children?
   Describe what you enjoyed about the book. (25)

6. Stories can teach us a great deal about life and relationships.
   Write about a fictional book which has taught you a valuable lesson. (25)

Exercise 2.5: Writing about pictures (1)

1.   Write about ONE of these pictures in an interesting way.   (25)

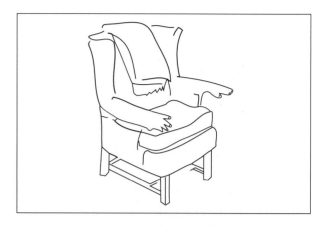

Exercise 2.6: Writing about pictures (2)

1. Write about ONE of these pictures in an interesting way. (25)

 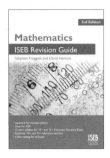  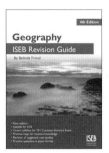
 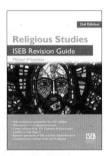